Black Americans

Black Americans

A PSYCHOLOGICAL ANALYSIS

E. Earl Baughman

The University of North Carolina at Chapel Hill

With a Foreword by M. Brewster Smith

ACADEMIC PRESS New York and London

ACADEMIC PRESS, INC.
111 Fifth Avenue, New York, New York 10003

United Kingdom Edition published by
ACADEMIC PRESS, INC. (LONDON) LTD.
Berkeley Square House, London W1X 6BA

LIBRARY OF CONGRESS CATALOG CARD NUMBER: 70-152748

PRINTED IN THE UNITED STATES OF AMERICA

To Barbara, Gretchen, and Elizabeth

Contents

Chapter 1. The Concept of Race

Chapter 2. Intelligence

Chapter 3. Scholastic Performance

Chapter 4. Self-Esteem

Chapter 5. Rage and Aggression

Foreword

Can Americans still think clearly about their most disruptive and most shameful problem, that of race? Can psychology and the social sciences still provide relevant evidence to answer open questions about our racial dilemmas, or must we resign ourselves to their being used solely to provide ammunition for positions dogmatically embraced? Do the urgencies of social justice, for belated moral action—or the defensive reactions of those who are threatened by new racial alignments—preempt the field, leaving no place for dispassionate inquiry?

I cannot be sanguine about the answers to these far-from-academic questions. Little has happened to falsify the grim prophecy of the Kerner Commission report, that we are far on the route to becoming a divided nation, white and black, beyond the reach of democratic compromise and irretrievably forsaking the ideals of the American Dream. Much has happened to suggest that America's obsession with race may have neared or passed the boundary beyond which the spirit of science, open-minded and evidential, can no longer contribute. When scientific disagreement leads to personal vilification, as it recently has in matters of race, we are dangerously close to the edge. As polarization heightens, facts become irrelevant. Motives become impugned, whole lines of evidence get read out of court.

In this context I particularly value this old-fashioned yet very modern book. It is old-fashioned in its liberal assumptions—that clear thought and scientific evidence are "relevant" to the correction of social injustice; that one may respect and, selectively, use the research and scholarship of psychologists with whose conclusions one does not fully agree; that, indeed, a white psychologist can write significantly about blacks. It would be good if we could take such old-fashioned qualities of reasonableness and good will for granted. We obviously cannot, in the difficult, con-flicted, guilt-ridden area of race and race relations in today's America.

This is also a very modern book. In it, Baughman draws heavily and appropriately on his collaborative monographic study with W. Grant Dahlstrom, *Negro and White Children: A Psychological Study in the Rural South* (1968), the most thorough and comprehensive comparative study that has thus far been carried out on its topic, a book that shares the virtues of the present one but is necessarily much less readable. It is also informed by wide acquaintance with the recent literature, and reports, along the way, some important new results that change my own thinking about the key topic of self-esteem in blacks and whites.

It is an honest and therefore controversial book, which prejudiced partisans ("prejudiced" in the literal sense of rigidly prejudging) will find hard to accept. Baughman ventures to give his own personal judgments of the recent controversial research literature and of social strategies, and these do not fit a stereotyped mold. Since the evidence on many points is still all too scanty and obscure, he may be wrong. But the reader's thinking about issues and evidence is bound to be clarified and enriched.

The neophyte whose initial guidance to the literature of race, black and white, comes from the text of this book and from the excellent selection of Suggested Readings will get a fair-minded introduction to a controversial field. In spite of Baughman's sensible discussion of the recent "Jensen controversy," however, the inexperienced reader may not sense what a rare thing such a reasonable book is in this emotionally charged field. Baughman cites Jensen, Deutsch, Pettigrew, and Shuey—all for positive contributions to our understanding. The reader is not told how unusual it has become for these authorities to rub shoulders together. If and as he pursues the readings that are recommended, he will discover virtues in the Baughman treatment that he had taken for granted.

The title of the book, *Black Americans*, reflects the now current terminology of American race relations. For me, it took extensive exposure to black people in Ghana and Nigeria before I realized the essential truth that the category "Negro" is an American creation, carrying for black and white alike the connotative freight of the American experience of black slavery and its aftermath. For almost any American, however prejudiced or enlightened, the category simply does not fit black Africans. Black Americans do well to seek to escape from it, and white people of good will to support them in doing so.

In the new semantics of race and ethnic membership, "black" is a self-chosen category, "Negro" an imposed one. Substitution of "black" for "Negro," while obviously desirable in a more mutually respectful racial etiquette, does give trouble in contexts such as much of the present book where, indeed, the consequences of the imposed category are under examination. Strictly speaking, much of the book is about *Negroes*, as defined by whites, Negroes who are still in the process of defining and choosing themselves as "blacks."

The book presents a selective, elementary treatment that introduces the reader to important issues and does not try to deal with them exhaustively. It should therefore be well suited as a supplementary text for a course in elementary psychology, or for schools of education. The facts and issues are ones that whites and blacks in many walks of life need to be familiar with. If more of us could keep our intellectual cool as well as Baughman does, we would be more likely to make lasting headway on the difficult problems that we face as blacks and whites. Just now there is no shortage of passion.

M. Brewster Smith

Preface

American psychologists have emphasized the importance of the environment in their studies of human behavior. Because the environment of the typical black American differs in a number of critical ways from that of the typical white American, one might expect that considerable attention would be focused upon blacks in both introductory and advanced textbooks in psychology. This is contrary to fact, however, as an examination of a random sample of such books will demonstrate. Blacks may be mentioned occasionally—usually in discussions of intelligence or prejudice—but one does not find a comprehensive psychological analysis of this important minority group in the most widely used textbooks.

It is clear, then, that while most psychologists probably would agree that black Americans have not received adequate treatment in many disciplines (history, for example), they have been slow to correct a similar imbalance in their own field. The primary motivation for writing this brief book was to see if I might not contribute to changing this situation at the undergraduate level of instruction. This book is addressed, therefore, to students in a variety of introductory psychology courses: general psychology, personality, child psychology, and so on. Because such courses are taught from so many different theoretical points of view, I have attempted to write simply and directly, avoiding "jargon" which might necessitate that the reader have an understanding of a particular theoretical system.

It is also my judgment that *Black Americans* could find a useful place in the curricula of most schools of education. My own experiences with public school teachers impress me with the fact that many of them—both black and white—are not familiar with most of the substantive material that is presented in the following pages, and in these days and times such a situation should not exist. It may even be that this book might serve a useful purpose for inservice training of teachers who are already coping with the many problems brought about by school desegregation. Some prepublication reviewers of the manuscript have gone even further and been so kind as to suggest that it would be valuable reading for any citizen who is concerned with the complex problems associated with race that abound in our contemporary society.

The reader may very well wonder what guided my selection of certain topics to discuss and my omission of others. The topics included are basically those which behavioral scientists have studied with reference to blacks to the point where a respectable body of research literature exists that can be drawn upon for a book such as this. Also, of course, these topics are, in my judgment, of critical importance if the psychological processes of black Americans are to be understood. The omission of certain other topics may be more difficult to justify. I have not, for example, made sexual behavior one of my focal topics. This decision was based primarily upon the fact that so much has already been written elsewhere about this subject matter and most Americans do understand that sex—particularly interracial sex—has greatly affected the relationships between blacks and whites in this country. While it is true that interracial dating has increased markedly on many of our campuses, it is also true that the incidence of interracial marriage has not increased at a comparable rate. Perhaps if a revision of this book is justified a few years hence, changes in our customs and attitudes in this area of behavior may argue then for the addition of sexual behavior as a major topic.

Neither have I discussed social attitudes and prejudice in a focused manner because, as noted earlier, this is one topic that is frequently covered in undergraduate textbooks. Also, *many* additional references to this subject are readily available to readers everywhere. I do, of course, give considerable attention throughout the book to how prejudice and discrimination affect the various behavior patterns developed by black Americans.

One final observation is in order. This book is not written from the "inside"; it does not do what only blacks can do—to tell us what it feels like to be a black in contemporary America. James Baldwin, Malcolm X, Ralph Ellison, and other blacks do a superb job in describing this experience, and any serious student of the black American should pay careful attention to the messages they send. But there are other perspectives that must also be considered, and I have attempted to cover the most important of these in this book. It is reassuring to me that black students—as well as white students—who have read this manuscript in my course on black personality do report that their psychological understanding of black Americans has been expanded by the experience.

Acknowledgments

Without the collaboration of W. Grant Dahlstrom in the research which led to the publication of *Negro and White Children: A Psychological Study in the Rural South,* the present book could not have been written. Also, both books are very much dependent upon the continued encouragement and unqualified support provided by the staff of Academic Press. I am deeply indebted and grateful to them, as well as to Eugene Long who helped make it possible for me to secure the time necessary to write such a book. David Galinsky also provided assistance which facilitated completion of the work.

Several individuals read initial drafts of the manuscript and provided me with valuable suggestions. In this regard, I especially want to recognize the contributions of Irwin Katz, Harold McCurdy, John Thibaut, Samuel Fillenbaum, Robert Brown, and W. Grant Dahlstrom. They are, of course, without responsibility for whatever defects may be found in the final product.

Preparation of the final copy was facilitated through the combined efforts of Blanche Critcher, Shirley Talley, Mary LoLordo, and Murie Dyer. Their assistance expedited my work and made it more enjoyable in variety of ways. The figures were drawn by Jeanne Hudson and reflect the excellence that her past work has taught me to expect.

Finally, several authors and publishers very kindly granted me permission to reproduce portions of their material.

All blacks are angry.

William H. Grier and Price M. Cobbs

Race naming may be somewhat arbitrary, but race differences are facts of nature which can be studied to help us understand the continuing evolution of man . . . . Racial differences are not signs of inferiority or superiority in themselves.

I. I. Gottesman

Chapter 1 / The Concept of Race

Americans live in a country in which a person's experience and behavior may be markedly influenced by his subgroup membership. Individuals who are white and middle class sometimes "overlook" this fact, but black Americans are acutely aware of it. Even blacks, however, may have a distorted or incomplete conception of how race membership is linked to experience and behavior. Our primary objective in this book is to describe this linkage to the extent that the social and behavioral sciences provide us with findings relevant to it.

Black, Negro, Afro-American, Colored?

The contemporary scene in the United States is a very fluid one as far as racial issues are concerned. One of its most salient characteristics, of course, is the increased assertiveness of the black population, which, by 1972, may constitute as much as one-eighth of the total population (U.S. Department of Labor, 1965). A fundamental goal of this assertive—even militant—activity by black Americans is the achievement of an identity which connotes pride, not inferiority.

For both individuals and groups, the achievement of a new or altered identity is extremely difficult. Some blacks believe they can achieve this

1

objective only by reestablishing their connections with African culture and history, connections that slavery almost completely destroyed. To call oneself an Afro-American is a constant reminder of this heritage and may indeed be helpful in the effort to build a new identity.

However, relatively few black Americans refer to themselves as Afro-Americans. In fact, if we can generalize from a study conducted in 1968 on Chicago's South Side (see Brieland, 1969), a majority of blacks prefer to be called Negroes. Among the more articulate and militant blacks, though, Negro is often rejected as the white man's term. They see Negro as having derogatory connotations, perhaps because it is sometimes mispronounced as "Nigra," a mispronunciation that suggests "Nigger."

The choice of an identifying term is a matter that blacks must and will settle for themselves. Our impression is that the trend is running increasingly in favor of "black," especially among the younger generation, and this is the term that we shall use in the discussion that follows.[1] However, there will be occasional exceptions to this general practice, usually when a citation from the literature makes use of the term "Negro."

Social versus Biological Definitions of Race

Biological scientists agree that all men belong to one species, *homo sapiens* ("wise man"). If Arthur Koestler and others are correct in suggesting that man may prove to be an evolutionary mistake, man's choice of a name for his species will seem to have been not only immodest (see Pettigrew, 1964, p. 59) but most inappropriate. This, however, is a judgment that the future will have to render.

In the biological sense, race has the status of a subspecies. How many races or subspecies are there? There is no agreed upon answer to this question; as Gottesman (1968) points out, the number of races that one identifies depends upon one's objectives. Thus, at the most general level, race can be defined so that virtually all of the earth's population can be assigned to one of ten races. At the other extreme, races may be much

[1] This represents a change in our own practice. In 1968, for example, we published a book with the title, *Negro and White Children: A Psychological Study in the Rural South* (W. Grant Dahlstrom, coauthor).

more narrowly defined so that they number in the thousands. Although many criteria have been used to differentiate races both broadly and narrowly, current biological classifications depend heavily upon differences in gene frequencies as determined by chemical analyses of blood samples. Biologists usually regard races as breeding populations and cite both geographical and cultural barriers as important reasons for their development.

The black American, in biological terms, is a hybrid produced by slaves—coming predominantly from western Africa—and European settlers. In biology, of course, cross-mating often produces a superior product, but racists refuse to consider such a possibility for *homo sapiens*. White racists, for example, express the fear that interracial reproduction will lead to "mongrelization" of what they call the white race. In point of fact, however, geneticists have shown that completely random mating of American whites and blacks would result in the virtual elimination of the black American as we now know him (see Stern, 1954; Pettigrew, 1964). This is so, of course, because black Americans comprise only slightly more than 10% of the total population, and most blacks already have significant numbers of white genes (see Gottesman, 1968). In the most basic sense, then, black racists have more to fear from a completely free mixing of the races than do white racists.

Both blacks and whites have accepted the custom of calling anyone "black" if they have even a trace of black ancestry, even though this is ridiculous from a biological point of view. The only exception in this regard seems to occur when the individual with black ancestry is so lacking in Negroid characteristics that he can pass as white, and chooses to do so. As far as individual experience is concerned, it is this social conception of race that is controlling, not the biological conception. Our concern, therefore, is with those persons who, in social terms, are declared to be members of the black population. And this social definition, as we know, depends almost completely upon a person's skin color.

Confounding Race and Social Class

It has long been recognized that at least three major social classes can be distinguished in the United States. Also, the evidence is overwhelming that blacks have a disproportionately high representation in the lower class. This imbalance in social class representation makes for great difficulty when researchers set out to analyze the relationships between race and behavior. When black–white differences in behavior are found, is race really the determining factor or is it a matter of social class variables? Frequently no clear-cut answer to this question is possible, and we are forced to describe a difference the cause of which is undetermined. In evaluating reported research, the reader must keep this intricate problem constantly in mind and be cautious in his interpretation of reported findings. We shall attempt to follow this advice in the pages that follow, although we must acknowledge in advance that it is frequently difficult to separate the racial–ethnic aspects of being black from the influence of social class membership.

The fact that being black means something more than social class standing, however, must also be emphasized and held constantly in mind. Malcolm X drives this point home in his autobiography when he describes his interaction with a middle-class black college professor (1965, p. 284):

> One particular university's "token-integrated" black Ph.D. asso-ciate professor I never will forget; he got me so mad I couldn't see straight. As badly as our 22 millions of educationally deprived black people need the help of any brains he has, there he was looking like some fly in the buttermilk among white "colleagues"—and he was trying to *eat me up!* He was ranting about what a "divisive demagogue" and what a "reverse racist" I was. I was racking my head, to spear that fool; finally I held up my hand, and he stopped. "Do you know what white racists call black Ph.D.'s?" He said something like, "I believe that I happen to be aware of that"—you know, one of those ultra-proper-talking Negroes. And I laid the word down on him, loud: "Nigger!"[2]

Achieving middle-class status, then, does not mean the same thing for the black man as it does for the white man—at least as far as a significant section of American society is concerned. He still must confront the fact that much of his experience is going to be affected by his color and that his racial identity goes with him no matter what socioeconomic level he manages to achieve.

[2] Copyright © 1964 by Alex Haley & Malcolm X; Copyright © 1965 by Alex Haley & Betty Shabazz; reprinted by permission of Grove Press, Inc.

Chapter 2 / Intelligence

Much of the bitter debate about the "nature" of the black American has focused upon his alleged intellective inferiority. This allegation, of course, has served as a rationalization for many forms of discriminatory treatment. In this section we shall examine some of the evidence concerning the black man's intellective power, its sources, and its modifiability.

Black—White Differences in IQ

Traditionally, a person's IQ has been regarded as an index of his general intellective power or capacity. Many tests, some group administered, others individually administered, have been developed to assess this capacity. A random sample of the general white population would be expected to have a mean IQ of 100 while approximately two-thirds of the sample should have IQ's between 85 and 115.

Many studies, using a wide variety of IQ tests, have been conducted over the years to compare black and white intelligence (see Shuey, 1966; also, Dreger & Miller, 1960, 1968). Although there is, as we would expect, some variation in results, the mean IQ for black samples generally falls close to 85, or approximately 15 points below the mean for white samples.

5

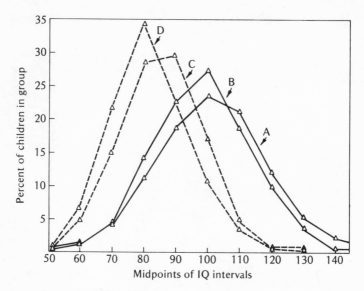

Fig. 1. Percentages of children from four research groups who earned various IQ scores. A = USA white children (N = 1419) (Terman & Merrill, 1937). B = Millfield white children (N = 464) and C = Millfield black children (N = 542) (Baughman & Dahlstrom, 1968). D = Southeast USA black children (N = 1630) (Kennedy, Van de Riet, & White, 1963). (From Baughman & Dahlstrom, 1968.)

The average IQ of blacks tends to be highest in the urban areas of the North and lowest in the rural areas of the deep South.

Figure 1 shows the percentages of children from four research groups (two black, two white) who earned various IQ scores on the Stanford–Binet Intelligence Scale (S–B), one of the widely used individual intelligence tests. Curve A is representative of white American schoolchildren; curves B and C are based upon white and black schoolchildren respectively living in "Millfield," a rural area in central North Carolina; and curve D is based upon black schoolchildren living in five southeastern states (Alabama, Georgia, Florida, South Carolina, and Tennessee). A very important point to note with respect to these curves is the substantial degree of overlap that exists between the two curves representing black samples and the two curves representing white samples. This means that significant numbers of black children earned IQ scores higher than those of white children even though the mean white scores exceed the mean black scores.

In thinking about intelligence, it is important to remember that intelligence is a hypothetical construct; that is, we develop a concept which we call intelligence in order to explain certain types of variations in observable behavior. Technically, the IQ is a measure of performance on specified tasks under standardized conditions. Although we use this measure of performance to make inferences about the hypothetical construct labeled intelligence, we must recognize that performance can be affected by a number of factors besides the basic intellective capacity of the person (see below). In short, the IQ can seldom be accepted as a "pure" reflection of intelligence alone.

1. Age and Sex Differences

It has frequently been asserted that the rate of intellective growth for blacks is less than that for whites, and that blacks reach their "ceiling" at an earlier age. Some observers are more specific; they believe that blacks level off or even begin to decline in intellective capacity with the onset of puberty, but show normal intellective growth prior to this age. Still others contend that blacks show a steady decrease in IQ as they grow older.

A number of studies do show a decrease in IQ for black children with advancing age (see, for example, Kennedy *et al.*, 1963). As Pettigrew[3] (1964, p. 113) points out, however, ". . . environmentally-deprived Caucasian groups reveal precisely the same phenomenon. . . ." Since most black groups that have been studied were also environmentally deprived, it is difficult to defend the thesis that race as such has anything to do with an inverse relationship between age and IQ.

The Millfield data (see above) were plotted to show how IQ and age are related for four groups: white boys, white girls, black boys, and black girls. (Millfield is a rural area in North Carolina that has little intellectual stimulation for either white or black children.) As Figure 2 shows, the mean IQ of the black boys does drop after age 10, but this is also true for white boys and white girls. Interestingly, it is not characteristic of the black girls. Thus, these recent data support Pettigrew's contention that age plots of mean IQ scores do not reflect the operation of a race-linked factor.

It is obvious from Figure 2, we believe, that white boys and white girls do not differ in mean IQ. However, there is a suggestion of a sex difference in favor of the girls among the black children. When the eight age levels are combined, this difference is less than two IQ points, which, practically

[3] From *A Profile of the Negro American* by Thomas F. Pettigrew, Copyright ©1964, by Litton Educational Publishing Inc., by permission of Van Nostrand Reinhold Company.

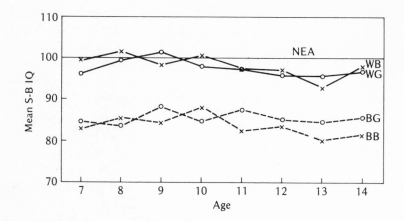

Fig. 2. Mean S–B IQ scores for each sex of each race at eight age levels. WB = white boys. WG = white girls. BB = black boys. BG = black girls. NEA = normal expectation for age. (From Baughman & Dahlstrom, 1968.)

speaking, has no significance. Furthermore, Kennedy's (1963) data from five southeastern states shows a mean IQ for black males that is about one-half point greater than that for females. In terms of measured intellective ability, then, we are on solid ground in concluding that there is no significant sex difference among either black or white children.

2. *The Genetic Explanation*

The existence of a gap in IQ between black and white children of both sexes is, as we have seen, a well-established empirical fact. But are genetic factors linked to race the determining consideration? *To this question there is as yet no satisfactory answer,* although there are tenaciously held opinions. First, we shall examine the genetic position.

To begin, it is clear that intelligence does have a genetic base. Behavioral geneticists also agree that intelligence is determined not by a single gene but by a number of genes acting independently to produce a cumulative result.[4] This genetic base, however, does not determine a specific IQ, which, we will remind the reader, is a measure of intellective *performance.* Instead, the genes determine a band or range within which

---

[4] In a recent analysis, Jinks and Fulker (1970, p. 343) conclude that "... at least 22 loci would seem to be controlling IQ."

an individual's IQ is likely to fall. The exact location of the IQ within this genetically determined range is dependent upon environmental factors which interact with the genetic factors in complex and as yet poorly understood ways.

The genetic position, then, does not argue that IQ is determined solely by hereditary factors; rather, it recognizes that intellective performance is also affected by environmental factors.[5] Therefore, the correct way to approach the problem at hand is to ask this question: How much of the variability in intelligence can be attributed to genetic factors and how much to environmental factors? Among human behavioral geneticists, the most widely accepted answer seems to be that approximately 80% of the variability in intelligence is due to genetic structure and 20% to environmental factors. These estimates are based upon a rather complicated mathematical analysis of data which show the correlations in IQ among individuals of different degrees of kinship—monozygotic twins, dizygotic twins, siblings, first cousins, and so on (see Cattell, 1965; Jensen, 1969).

Because a large number of empirical studies have consistently demonstrated a black—white gap in IQ, because hereditary factors apparently control such a large percentage of the variability in IQ scores, and because compensatory education programs (see pp. 16—19) have not eliminated the black—white gap, some researchers conclude that this gap is significantly influenced by genetic differences between the races which favor whites.

Jensenism. Until recently, however, the genetic interpretation of racial differences in IQ appeared to be in disrepute among most scientists despite its continued acceptance in certain sectors of the general population. The environmentalists (see pp. 10—11) were not only quite vocal, but they controlled the official statements made on race by organizations like the Society for the Psychological Study of Social Issues (see Albee *et al.,* 1969). Then, in 1969, Arthur R. Jensen, a highly respected educational psychologist on the University of California campus at Berkeley, published a lengthy article with the title "How Much Can We Boost IQ and Scholastic Achievement?" The fury created by this article probably is unequalled in the recent history of the behavioral sciences; some writers in the popular press already refer to its major thesis as "jensenism" (see

---

[5] The same conclusion is valid for many of a person's attributes, physical as well as behavioral. A person's genes, for example, help to determine his height, but so does his diet.

Edson, 1969). What is "jensenism," and why did it create such an uproar?

Jensenism, in its simplest terms, is essentially the genetic explanation of racial differences in IQ that we have just sketched. Jensen marshals, first of all, diverse evidence to support the thesis that IQ is determined primarily by the genes. Then, although he does not deny that environmental factors contribute to black–white differences in IQ, he concludes that genetic factors cannot be ignored as significant determinants of the gap. And he goes on to argue that because intelligence is locked in by biological factors, efforts to substantially increase the black IQ by programs of compensatory education (such as Headstart) are doomed to failure.

Pushing aside for the moment Jensen's judgment of compensatory education, let us insist that there is, basically, nothing new in Jensen's doctrine of a genetic basis for racial differences in IQ. What gives his article its distinct position, we believe, is the fact that it is the most penetrating and sophisticated presentation of the genetic position that has been made. Jensen obviously knows social science research in this area, and he understands human behavioral genetics; consequently, it is impossible to ignore him or dismiss him as a simple-minded, uninformed racist.[6] In Jensen the environmentalists have found a worthy opponent. Moreover, his central thesis is immediately threatening to many individuals— professionals and nonprofessionals alike—who have committed themselves to a solution of our racial problems based upon the belief that there are no racial differences in innate intellective capacity.

3. The Environmental Explanation

But how can racial differences in IQ be explained if Jensen is wrong and genetic factors are not responsible? Many possible nongenetic determinants of the black–white gap have been cited (see Dreger & Miller, 1968; Kagan, Hunt, Crow, Bereiter, Elkind, Cronbach, & Brazziel, 1969), although all are not equally relevant to each study reported in the literature. For example, Kennedy, and his associates (1963), in studying southeastern black children, used white male examiners whereas Baughman and Dahlstrom in their Millfield study used black female examiners to test

[6] However, it is possible for some experts to disagree with Jensen about the statistical assumptions involved in his calculation of the heritability index (see, for example, Light & Smith, 1969). But this issue remains unresolved since other competent geneticists do agree with the basic soundness of Jensen's analysis (see, for example, Crow, 1969).

black children and white female examiners to test white children (see pp. 14–15). It is possible—but not proved—that the lower mean score obtained in the Kennedy study for black children, as compared to the Millfield blacks, is due to the race and sex of the examiners used by Kennedy and his staff.

Although such factors as the race of the examiner may be relevant to the interpretation of particular studies, they cannot serve as adequate explanations for the racial differences found in many of the better conducted studies. The nongenetic explanation of these differences focuses instead upon two factors: the impoverished cultural and educational backgrounds of blacks and the limitations of the available intelligence tests. The Council of the Society for The Psychological Study of Social Issues, in a reply to Jensen's article, put it this way (see Albee et al., 1969, p. 1039):

> The evidence of four decades of research on this problem can be readily summarized. There are marked differences in intelligence test scores when one compares a random sample of whites and Negroes. What is equally clear is that little definitive evidence exists that leads to the conclusion that such differences are innate. The evidence points overwhelmingly to the fact that when one compares Negroes and whites of comparable cultural and educational background, differences in intelligence test scores diminish markedly; the more comparable the background, the less the difference. There is no direct evidence that supports the view that there is an innate difference between members of different racial groups.
>
> We believe that a more accurate understanding of the contribution of heredity to intelligence will be possible only when social conditions for all races are equal and when this situation has existed for several generations. . . . We must also recognize the limitations of present-day intelligence tests. Largely developed and standardized on white middle class children, these tests tend to be biased against black children to an unknown degree.

The line is drawn by the environmentalists, then, in terms of two basic issues. Not only are the commonly used measuring instruments inadequate, but no fair racial comparisons can be made—even if acceptable measuring devices are developed—until equal social conditions have been experienced by both races for several generations.

4. Family Correlates of IQ

A question that is of both theoretical and practical interest is this: Is there a type of information about a child's family that will permit us to predict how well he is likely to perform on intelligence tests? Numerous studies have given an affirmative answer to this question; usually the type of information that is so relevant reflects the socioeconomic status of the family. Thus, after investigating a number of family variables, the authors of the Millfield study reached the following conclusion (see Baughman & Dahlstrom, 1968, pp. 104–105):

> Thus we would suggest that most of these findings correspond quite well with the hypothesis that the intellective proficiency of the children is positively correlated with the socioeconomic status of the family from which they come. Pupils whose parents are better educated, whose fathers have obtained some position outside of farming, whose parents are able to buy their own homes and subscribe to services such as telephones, and whose parents have had relatively few children do better on such tests of ability and achievement than do less favored children.

Other studies have reached a similar conclusion. But the Millfield research, in addition, shows that the strength of the relationships between family variables and intellective performance are *lower* among the black children than among the white. Probably this finding results from the greater homogeneity that is found among the black families with respect to socioeconomic status and does not represent a true racial difference in how socioeconomic factors are related to intellective performance.

5. A Personal View

The criticism of existing intelligence tests in terms of bias against black children[7] has been, we believe, overly severe. While any such bias should be eliminated, we doubt that the accomplishment of this goal will substantially change the comparative data now available. The alteration of

[7] A comparable charge has been made that these tests are biased against lower-class white children, thus underestimating their intelligence as compared to that of middle-class white children.

social conditions to provide racial equity, however, is quite another matter. It is clear that the average black grows up under social conditions less conducive to optimal intellective development than the average white, and elimination of this inequity can only result in a reduction of the black–white gap in measured intelligence. We do not know if the gap would be eliminated entirely in a society in which social conditions were equal for all races, but its social significance surely would be greatly diminished. While the pure environmentalists probably underestimate the power of the methods that have been developed by the human behavioral geneticists, their emphasis on the social determinants of intelligence makes sense in the context of a commitment to the creation of a just society. We can insist upon an environment that is fair to all, but we cannot do much about our genes.[8]

Until a just society is realized, the black man is going to continue to be burdened by IQ data of the type that we have examined. As a person, therefore, it is essential for him to recognize the significance of overlap in IQ distributions plotted with respect to the social definition of race (see p. 6). Such data show that it is impossible to predict an individual's IQ by the color of his skin, and it is unfair to him to make predictions about his intelligence based upon differences in means between racial groups. Furthermore, actual achievements, either in school or in the world of work, depend on many personal qualities in addition to intelligence. (And there is even less evidence for a genetic basis for most of these qualities than there is for intelligence.) The black man must, therefore, fight against the unfair application of comparative IQ data while seeking social conditions which will provide him with equal opportunities to develop all of his potential qualities, both intellective and nonintellective.

Stability of the IQ

The discussion thus far indicates that an individual's IQ may be a function of his life circumstances; even those who emphasize the genetic basis of intelligence acknowledge that this is true. The question, then, is not whether the IQ may change but *how much* the IQ may change from

---

[8] R. T. Brown has pointed out (in a personal communication) "that in the best of all possible worlds all variability in intelligence would be ascribed to variability in genes." That is, each individual would live in what for him was the optimal environment for actualizing the potentials within him.

one testing session to another, and what conditions produce gains, losses, or no change at all in IQ. We shall examine this problem for black children now, citing empirical data, and referring—for comparative purposes—to comparable studies of white children when they are available. Changes in IQ under natural conditions will be considered, as well as changes when attempts are deliberately made to elevate the IQ's of children.

1. Measurement Errors

Before addressing the central questions, let us point out that we must be cautious about accepting the results of one administration of an intelligence test as a valid indicator of the testee's intelligence. These measurements are subject to several sources of error that may produce an IQ that is either too high or too low for the testee, although the latter outcome is probably most common. If the examiner is inexperienced, for example, he may inadvertently help or hinder the testee's performance. Even if the examiner is experienced, he may fail to develop rapport with a particular testee so that the latter's performance is affected. Sometimes a subject's lack of motivation is so deeply embedded that even the most experienced examiner who makes every effort to develop a comfortable working relationship with the subject fails to elicit a performance that is indicative of his ability. This motivational problem is especially acute in testing black children, many of whom have become accustomed to failure and who have received little or no reinforcement on those occasions when they have tried to do well. Before using an IQ score in a decision-making process, therefore, the possible effect of such factors should be carefully considered.

2. Changes in IQ among Young Black Children under Natural Conditions

If competent examiners test a group of subjects on two different occasions—even if several years separate these two testing sessions—the mean IQ score for the group will probably be about the same on the two occasions. From this observation one might be tempted to conclude that the IQ is stable, and, of course, it is—*for the group*. This group stability, however, usually hides a significant degree of individual variability which becomes apparent only if the scores of individual subjects on the two occasions are examined.

TABLE I

*Frequencies of S−B IQ Changes for Black Children,
1961-62 to 1964-65[a]*

Change in IQ	Boys	Girls
15−19	1	
10−14	2	6
5−9	4	4
1−4	5	3
0	2	2
(−1)−(−4)	5	3
(−5)−(−9)	6	7
(−10)−(−14)	0	3
(−15)−(−19)	2	
(−20)−(−24)	1	
(−25)−(−29)	1	
N	29	28
Mean	−1.9	+.8

[a]Based upon data from Baughman and Dahlstrom (1968).

To define the degree of this individual variation among young black children more precisely, let us cite data gathered in the Millfield study. Two experienced black female examiners tested 57 children (29 boys) at age 7 and again approximately 3 years later at age 10 using the Stanford−Binet Intelligence Scale (S−B). As Table I shows, 37 of these children (approximately two-thirds of the group) obtained an IQ on their second test that differed by at least 5 points from their score on the first test. The scores of 16 children changed by as much as 10 points.[9] Children who gained in IQ were balanced by those who lost so that, overall, the mean IQ's on the two occasions were almost identical.

Why are these data important? First, they demonstrate that we should hesitate to take one IQ score as *the* measure of a child's intelligence. Second, they force us to consider the question of why some children improve in intellective performance while others show a decrement with advancing age, a question that we shall return to below. The IQ's of black children are open to change, even under conditions where no special

[9] As Baughman and Dahlstrom show (1968, pp. 112-113), the statistical concept of "regression toward the mean" cannot be invoked as a full explanation of these changes in IQ.

efforts are being made to change them. Surely this should encourage us to believe that specially designed educational programs could prevent IQ losses and enhance gains.[10]

3. Attempts to Produce IQ Gains

The evidence now available, however, is discouraging as far as engineering gains in IQ is concerned. Much of the effort to accomplish this aim has focused upon intensive preschool programs for disadvantaged children (both black and white), but some has involved special approaches to teaching children in the regular school system. The gains in IQ produced by most of these programs have been modest; moreover, many of the gains have not persisted very long after the children have graduated from the special programs and entered regular school classes.

To illustrate how difficult it is to increase IQ's, let us return to the Millfield study. As part of this research program, a kindergarten was established at one of the two black schools in Millfield and also at one of the two white schools. Children were enrolled for full school days for the entire academic year. Three classes at each school during successive school years (1962–1963, 1963–1964, 1964–1965) were tested on the Stanford–Binet Intelligence Scale when they entered the kindergarten and again at the end of the year. No kindergartens were established at the other two schools, but children of kindergarten age in these two school districts were also tested twice (in the fall and spring of the year) so that they could serve as control subjects for the children enrolled in the kindergartens. The question, then, is whether the kindergarten children showed more intellective growth than the nonkindergarten children.

During the three years the 80 black children who attended the kindergarten showed a mean gain of 1.1 IQ points while the 74 black children who did not attend had a mean loss of .2 of an IQ point (see Figure 3 for a plot of these data). Statistically, this is not a significant difference, and, in practical terms, the difference cannot be regarded as meaningful. The 83 white kindergarten children, however, had a mean gain of 7.3 IQ points which is significantly higher than the mean gain of 2.0 IQ

[10] Unfortunately, Baughman and Dahlstrom were unable to conduct a similar study of young white children in Millfield. Therefore, we do not know if data for white children would be different from those for black children.

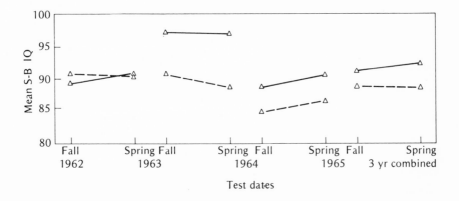

Fig. 3. Mean S–B IQ scores of black kindergarten (Δ—Δ) and nonkindergarten (Δ—·—Δ) children in fall and spring (three years separately and when the three classes are combined into one group for comparative purposes). (From Baughman & Dahlstrom, 1968.)

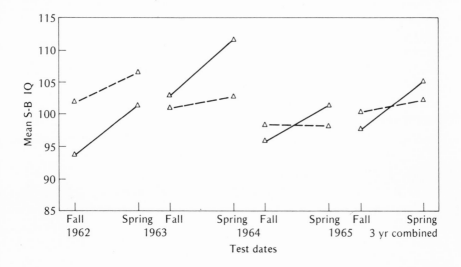

Fig. 4. Mean S–B IQ scores of white kindergarten (Δ—Δ) and nonkindergarten (Δ— —Δ) children in fall and spring (three years separately and when the three classes are combined into one group for comparative purposes). (From Baughman & Dahlstrom, 1968.)

points achieved by the 73 white nonkindergarten children (these data are plotted in Figure 4). In this instance, then, a kindergarten program appears to have stimulated a modest degree of intellective growth among the white children but not among the black. The result, of course, was a widening of the black—white gap in IQ.

This discouraging finding is offset somewhat, however, by the results obtained from another test—the Primary Mental Abilities Test (PMA)—which was administered to the same children using the same research design that has already been described for the S—B. Data from this test indicate that the rate of intellective growth for black kindergarten children matched that for white kindergarten children; also, that both groups showed significant gains over their nonkindergarten controls. Indeed, the black kindergarten children gained more in comparison with their control subjects than the white kindergarten children, a finding which is the reverse of that described above for the S—B.

We see, then, one more complication in evaluating the effects of interventional programs on intellective growth: Our conclusions may be dependent on the instrument we use to measure intelligence. In the Millfield study, for example, the PMA apparently was more sensitive to the intellective changes that were taking place in the kindergarten children, particularly those who were black. If only the S—B test had been used, significant intellective changes among the black children would have gone unrecognized.

Even though there is some encouragement in the PMA data, it is limited. Given the fact that these children attended school for a full day, five days per week, for the entire school year, the amount of intellective growth by any measure must be considered modest. This is one reason why we are very skeptical of reports in the mass media that a program like Headstart results in an average IQ gain of eight to ten points (see, for example, "Poverty," 1966), particularly when the research design producing such findings is not described.

The Millfield study is only one study, of course, and it provides no final answers in this domain. However, its results are not markedly out of line with other interventional efforts, a number of which are identified and evaluated in Jensen's 1969 article. Although we are not as pessimistic as Jensen is about the possiblity of engineering IQ gains ("The techniques for raising intelligence per se . . . probably lie more in the province of the biological sciences than in psychology and education."), we must agree that attempts to achieve this end so far have not been very successful.[11] On the other hand, Jensen and like-minded critics should, in our judgment, place greater emphasis on the fact that all attempts to produce IQ gains by environmental manipulation have been limited in scope. We have not as yet launched a full-scale effort in this direction which would give us a true indication of what is possible in this regard. Such a program would begin with prenatal care, attend carefully to the environmental stimulation provided the baby during his first year or two of life, and follow this with an educational program for the preschool years based upon what we now know about the learning process. Programs structured along these lines, and using control subjects, must be established before the limits of our power to produce IQ gains by structuring the environment can be determined.[12]

4. Correlates of IQ Change

A question that has not been extensively investigated is whether there are factors in a child's behavioral repertoire or family that relate to the IQ *change* he shows over a period of time. The Millfield researchers did study this problem in the context of evaluating how kindergarten training affects intellective development (see pp. 16–18), but they were unable to come up with positive findings for either black or white children. They were more successful, however, when they analyzed the intellective changes in black children between ages seven and ten (again, see pp.14–16). For these children there were a few family variables which related to their IQ changes, but most significant were the personal characteristics of the children themselves as determined by teachers' ratings of their behavior (Baughman & Dahlstrom, 1968, p. 127):

> The first-grade Negro child who is most likely to accelerate in intellective development tends to have a number of salient characteristics, as he is viewed by his teacher. He is self-sufficient, works hard at his lessons, sticks to the job, doesn't need much encouragement,

---

[11] While it is true that a few programs have produced encouraging gains in IQ, most of these gains have either disappeared upon termination of the program or at least decreased markedly.

[12] For a penetrating analysis of this problem and an optimistic outlook on what such programs might accomplish, consult the article written by J. McV. Hunt (1968, pp. 293-336).

and is consistent. As a person, he is warm, cooperative, trustful, and relatively free of anxiety. He is somewhat reactive to experiences of success and failure, especially success, and his teacher finds him an easy person to like.

Perhaps it is reasonable to summarize these findings by saying that the child who gains in IQ shows a greater degree of personal maturity than the child who does not. A prominent component of this maturity is a motivational factor involving a commitment to achieve or do well in learning situations.

This conclusion, of course, needs to be replicated in other studies. If it should hold up, it suggests that intellective development may be facilitated in children by structuring their experiences so as to build the types of personal attributes noted above. Perhaps in the long run this may prove to be a more effective approach to intellective development than an emphasis on early intellective training per se.

Primary Mental Abilities

As a measure of general intelligence, IQ tests have proved their value. It has long been recognized, however, that it is also useful to differentiate a number of *specific* mental abilities. These abilities correlate positively with one another and with IQ, yet they also define a variety of distinctive mental processes. For example, the ability to work with numbers is distinguished from the ability to understand words. Much of the pioneer work in defining these abilities was inspired by an eminent American psychologist, L. L. Thurstone, who called them *primary* mental abilities.

Although black—white comparisons in the intellective domain have focused upon IQ scores, tests devised to measure the primary mental abilities give us the opportunity to approach this problem more analytically. Again, for illustrative purposes, let us turn to the Millfield study. Children in this study whose IQ's were measured by the Stanford—Binet Intelligence Scale also took Thurstone's Primary Mental Abilities Test (PMA). The PMA is composed of five subtests which measure five abilities: (1) *Verbal Meaning,* or the ability to understand words; (2) *Perceptual Speed,* or the ability to recognize similarities and differences in pictorially presented objects; (3) *Number Facility,* or the ability to solve number

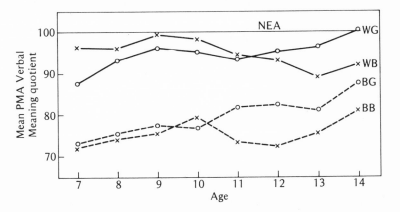

Fig. 5. Mean PMA Verbal Meaning quotients for each sex of each race at eight age levels. WB = white boys. WG = white girls. BB = black boys. BG = black girls. NEA = normal expectation for age. (From Baughman & Dahlstrom, 1968.)

problems and understand quantitative relationships; (4) *Spatial Relations,* or the ability to recognize relationships among geometric forms; and (5) *Reasoning,* or the ability to solve a variety of problems by the reasoning process. The results on three of the PMA's subtests—Verbal Meaning, Number Facility, and Spatial Relations—are plotted according to the age, sex, and race of the subjects in Figures 5, 6, and 7, respectively.

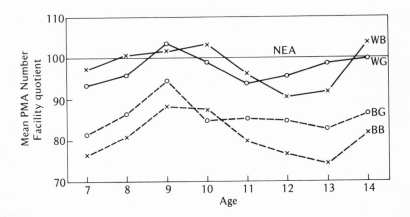

Fig. 6. Mean PMA Number Facility quotients for each sex of each race at eight age levels. WB = white boys. WG = white girls. BB = black boys. BG = black girls. NEA = normal expectation for age. (From Baughman & Dahlstrom, 1968.)

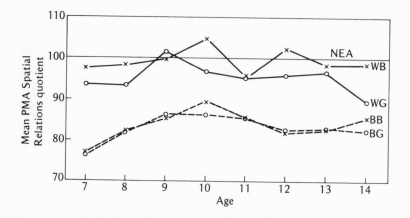

Fig. 7. Mean PMA Spatial Relations quotients for each sex of each race at eight age levels. WB = white boys. WG = white girls. BB = black boys. BG = black girls. NEA = normal expectation for age. (From Baughman & Dahlstrom, 1968.)

As Figure 5 shows, the black children enter school markedly deficient —compared to the white children—in their ability to understand words. At the eighth-grade level there is still a significant racial gap, but it has been narrowed appreciably. The gain of the black girls during these years is especially impressive; by ages 13 and 14 they are almost equal to white boys in their ability to understand words. It is also clear, however, that black boys lag considerably behind black girls at the older age levels. In other words, there are significant racial, sex, and age differences in this ability.

The picture with respect to number facility is quite different from that for verbal meaning, as we can see by comparing Figure 6 with Figure 5. Again, there is a substantial racial difference, but there is no systematic change with age. Moreover, there is a sex difference in favor of the girls beginning at the lowest age level among the black children but not among the white children. Thus, during the elementary school years there is no meaningful change in the black–white gap in number facility, nor is there a substantial change in the sex differential among the black children which favors the girls.

Finally, the pattern for spatial ability (see Figure 7) differs from both verbal meaning and number facility. Like verbal meaning, there is a narrowing of the black–white gap with advancing age; however, there is no sex difference among the black children at either the older or younger age levels. The lack of a sex difference for the black children is especially interesting since there is one for the white children—in favor of the boys. This is the only ability measured by the PMA, incidentally, for which there is a sex difference for either race that favors the boys.

The importance of these data is to be found, we believe, in the fact that the racial, sex, and age differences do vary according to the ability measured and in ways that could not be anticipated from the plot of IQ scores (see Figure 2, p. 8). If we can adequately understand why these differences come about under natural conditions, we should enhance our power to intervene for the purpose of enhancing the development of specific abilities. This is a more molecular approach to intellective development than one which focuses simply upon IQ changes.

The findings of the Millfield study with respect to various mental abilities are in essential agreement with results reported earlier by Lesser, Fifer, and Clark (1965) in a comparative study of six- and seven-year-old children from different social and cultural backgrounds (Negro, Jewish, Puerto Rican, and Chinese). These researchers focused upon four mental abilities (verbal, reasoning, number facility, and space conceptualization). Among their conclusions was the following statement (1965, p. 82): "Differences in *ethnic-group* membership *do* produce significant differences in *both* the absolute *level* of each mental ability and the *patterns* among these abilities." Thus, the Millfield study does not stand alone; rather, it reinforces the validity of previous findings and underscores our suggestion made above that we need to discover what factors are responsible for producing these ethnic differences in specific mental abilities.

Chapter 3/Scholastic Performance

Jensen, in his controversial article, concludes that scholastic performance is determined less by heredity than is intelligence.[13] He also suggests that educators should concentrate more upon enhancing scholastic performance and less upon IQ gains (1969, p. 108):

> The evidence so far suggests the tentative conclusion that the pay-off of preschool and compensatory programs in terms of IQ gains is small. Greater gains are possible in scholastic performance when instructional techniques are intensive and highly focused. . . . Educators would probably do better to concern themselves with teaching basic skills directly than with attempting to boost overall cognitive development. By the same token, they should deemphasize IQ tests as a means of assessing gains, and use mainly direct tests of the skills the instructional program is intended to inculcate.

Although we may not fully agree with Jensen's pessimistic position on boosting "overall cognitive development," his observation is helpful in that

[13]Scholastic performance and IQ are positively correlated, and IQ tests do a reasonably good job of predicting academic achievement. Obviously, however, scholastic performance is influenced by a number of factors other than intelligence, motivation being probably the most important one.

it reminds us that preschool and compensatory programs are not necessarily without value if they fail to effect IQ gains. Also, he may be right in advising that educators should focus upon what they know best, that is, how to develop basic skills—at least until researchers have learned how to produce IQ gains.

Race, Sex, and Age Differences

In any event, let us take a brief look at the scholastic performance of black children as compared to that of white children; such comparisons are usually made on the basis of scores secured on standard academic achievement tests, of which there are many available. As with intelligence, it will be instructive to consider sex and age differences within each race.

The black–white gap in scholastic performance varies, of course, from one school setting to the next. On the average, however, this gap is of approximately the same magnitude as is found when intelligence is measured (see Coleman et al., 1966). To illustrate this fact—as well as others—we shall return once again to the Millfield study.[14]

The Stanford Achievement Test (SAT) was administered to all of Millfield's children in grades one through eight. This test consists of six subtests: Paragraph Meaning, Word Meaning, Spelling, Language, Arithmetic Reasoning, and Arithmetic Computation. In addition to separate scores on each of these subtests, an overall score—called the Battery Median—is computed for each child.

Figure 8 shows the mean Battery Median scores at each of eight ages for white boys, white girls, black boys, and black girls. As other studies would lead us to predict, the mean scores of the black children are consistently below those of the white children and, in absolute terms, the gap grows wider with advancing age. Of additional interest is the fact that the overall scholastic performance of the black girls is better than that of the black boys *at every age level;* moreover, the gap between the black girls

---

[14]The reader may ask why we do not focus here upon the Coleman report instead of the Millfield study. Our primary reason is that we were able to apply more stringent controls to the gathering of the Millfield data than Coleman and his associates were able to use in the short time period available to them for completing their research. The Coleman study has, of course, been widely reported and debated in both the mass media and in scholarly publications. For a complete report of the Millfield study, see Baughman and Dahlstrom, 1968.

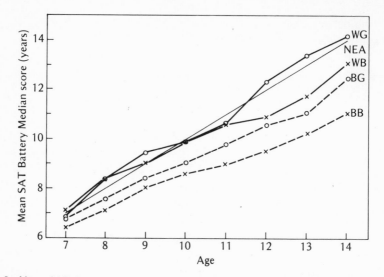

Fig. 8. Mean SAT Battery Median scores for each sex of each race at eight age levels. WB = white boys. WG = white girls. BB = black boys. BG = black girls. NEA = normal expectation for age. (From Baughman & Dahlstrom, 1968.)

and the white boys is small, especially at the upper age levels. (Incidentally, the fact that the white boys perform poorly at the upper age levels compared to white girls *cannot* be attributed to lower intelligence; as we saw in Figure 2, p. 8, there is no difference in their mean IQ's at these ages.)[15]

Mean scores on the Paragraph Meaning subtest—which measures a child's understanding of paragraphs that he reads—are plotted in Figure 9. The pattern for the black children is similar to the one shown in Figure 8, except that the departure from normal expectation with advancing age is greater. Relatively speaking, the black children do better on the Word Meaning subtest, which measures the knowledge of separate words rather than comprehension of connected discourse (this plot is not shown; it is very similar to Figure 8). This is particularly true at the older ages where the mean scores on Word Meaning are closer to normal expectation than are the mean scores on Paragraph Meaning.

[15] Data like these support, we believe, the argument that both ability *and* achievement tests should be included in a full assessment program. There are those who defend the thesis that ability tests are *only* achievement tests, but the evidence suggests otherwise. They do overlap, to be sure, but they are not completely interchangeable.

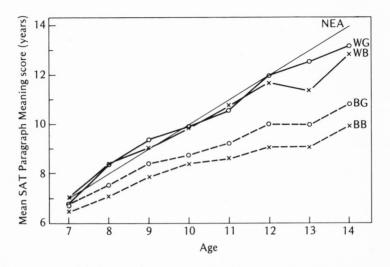

Fig. 9. Mean SAT Paragraph Meaning scores for each sex of each race at eight age levels. WB = white boys. WG = white girls. BB = black boys. BG = black girls. NEA = normal expectation for age. (From Baughman & Dahlstrom, 1968.)

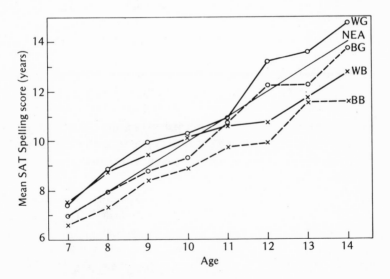

Fig. 10. Mean SAT Spelling scores for each sex of each race at eight age levels. WB = white boys. WG = white girls. BB = black boys. BG = black girls. NEA = normal expectation for age. (From Baughman & Dahlstrom, 1968.)

The results for the Spelling subtest, however, are quite different (see Figure 10). Especially remarkable is the performance of the black girls when one keeps in mind their average IQ (see Figure 2). These girls spell very close to the national average at every age level, and at the older ages their performance definitely exceeds that of the white boys even though their average IQ is significantly lower. The results for the Language subtest are less dramatic (the plot of these scores is not shown), yet beginning with age 11 there is no significant difference in the performance of black girls and white boys. (The Language subtest measures the child's accuracy in capitalization, punctuation, sentence sense, language usage, and knowledge of grammar.)

The child's success in reasoning in arithmetic terms is measured by the Arithmetic Reasoning subtest. The plot of scores for this subtest is not shown, but it is highly similar to that of the Battery Median scores (see Figure 8, p. 26). The same conclusion holds for performance on the Arithmetic Computation subtest, except that black girls and white boys show less difference at the older age levels than on the Arithmetic Reasoning subtest.

We believe that these findings are important for several reasons. First, they demonstrate the importance of examining not only overall scholastic performance but achievement in specific academic areas. (Remember, of course, that we reached a comparable conclusion with respect to intelligence.) Second, they justify the maintenance of a distinction between achievement and intelligence. If achievement had not been measured, for example, the superiority of black girls to white boys (or their equality) in certain skill areas would not have been detected. Third, it is clear that below average ability, as measured by IQ tests, does not necessarily "doom" a group to subnormal performance in all academic skill areas. High motivation—which other evidence suggested was characteristic of the black girls—for example, can elevate performance above the level suggested as likely by IQ tests.

One more observation based upon the differential performance of the black girls on the subtests of the SAT is in order. Their strongest performances seem to occur when memory processes are critical in producing success on test items. Thus, they do extremely well on Spelling, and comparatively well on identifying the correct meaning of individual words. Their poorest performance, in contrast, occurs when they are asked to determine the meaning of connected discourse, a task in which memory per se appears to be less critical.

Scholastic Performance and IQ Level

It is sometimes asserted that black children who, relative to their own group, have high intelligence fail to perform in school at a level in keeping with their ability. Is this true? One way to investigate this question is to compare the performance levels of black and white children who have been matched on IQ. This was done in the Millfield study not for one ability level but for four: children with S—B IQ's less than 80; those with IQ's in the 80—89 range; those in the 90—99 range; and, lastly, those in the 100—109 range. Academic performance was determined by the SAT as we have already described.

The results of this study are plotted in Figure 11, separately for each IQ group and according to the ages of the children.[16] As the plot in the upper left-hand quadrant shows, the overall scholastic performance of the relatively bright black children is consistently below that of the white children of comparable ability. Furthermore, when the SAT data are analyzed separately for each of its six subtests, the conclusion is the same. That is, on each of the subtests the white children in the 100—109 IQ range outperform their black counterparts.

At the intermediate IQ levels (that is, between 80 and 99), there is no consistent racial difference in scholastic performance. But at the lowest IQ level (below 80) it is very interesting to find that the racial difference is the reverse of that described above for the 100—109 IQ group: after age 7, the black children consistently outperform the white children of equal ability. Admittedly, this difference is small, yet we cannot ignore the fact that at every age level it favors the black children.

These data suggest, we believe, that the work in the black classrooms is directed more to the low ability child. It may even be that their black teachers have gained a certain expertise in teaching them that surpasses the competence of white teachers. Some observers would predict, we believe, that dull white children would have their intellective growth stimulated simply by being immersed in classrooms with many able peers, but the Millfield data do not accord with such a prediction. Very clear, however, is the fact that the relatively able black children are falling short of their potential—if the performance level of white children with comparable ability is used as a referent. If the efforts of the black teachers are directed

[16]The 100-109 IQ group was divided into only four age levels in order to have the black groups sufficiently large to provide stable mean SAT scores.

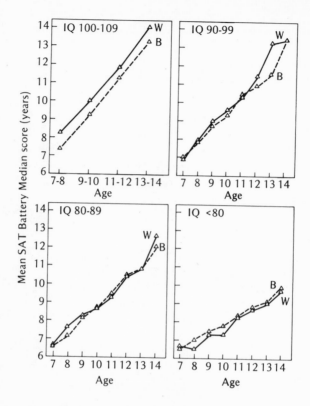

Fig. 11. Mean SAT Battery Median scores for white (W) and black (B) children at four IQ levels and various age levels. (From Baughman & Dahlstrom, 1968.)

primarily toward the lower ability levels, the brighter black children should show the type of decrement that is apparent in these data.

Family Correlates of Scholastic Performance

It has been generally established that a number of variables which are indicative of a family's socioeconomic status correlate positively with children's scholastic performance and IQ's, as we noted earlier. In the Millfield study, these relationships were stronger for the white children than for the black children. They also tended to be greater for some of the measures of academic achievement than for the measures of intelligence.

The Effects of School Desegregation

A central concern of blacks and whites alike during recent years has been the effect that desegregation of the public schools will have upon the scholastic performance of children. The leadership in the black community has tended to view desegregation in positive terms, that is, as a way of providing black children with a better school environment that would enhance their intellective growth. The black masses have been somewhat more ambivalent about the desirability of complete desegregation, although it is clear that they want their children to have the *right* to attend any school. The white leadership has been split, some leaders pushing strongly for full integration (not just desegregation) and others fighting by every means available to preserve a dual school system. The white masses, like the black, have had their reservations about desegregation; the concern that they have emphasized most has centered on the fear that their children would receive an inferior education.

As yet we do not have definitive evidence that either the hopes or fears of the various groups are realized when a segregated school system is replaced by a desegregated system. Research on this problem is extremely difficult to carry out, as Irwin Katz (1968, pp. 254–289) has recently demonstrated in a review and analysis of the relevant data that are available. One problem, for example, is the fact that the black children who desegregate a particular white school often are not representative of the total population of black children in the school district. Another problem is that desegregation frequently does not mean what it seems to mean. Thus, if we go into a desegregated school we may find that many classes are all-black or all-white (or nearly so), indicating that a segregated approach to education has been maintained under a single roof. Such a situation hardly presents a fair test of how desegregation affects the scholastic performance of black children.

The evidence that is available *suggests* that desegregation—as it is now practiced—probably functions to the advantage of some black children and to the disadvantage of others. The attitudes and motivations of the individual black child are certainly important determinants of how he responds to this new experience, but so are components of the school situation. If the white children reject him socially, for example, it is likely that he will have greater difficulty taking advantage of the learning opportunities than if he finds acceptance and encouragement. Also, the attitudes of teachers and other school personnel can be critical. Since the academic standards of most black schools are below those of white schools, teaching personnel must be realistic about the level of competence that students from these schools bring to the desegregated school; otherwise, the inability of many black students to compete effectively with their white classmates may have a devastating influence upon the scholastic performance of the black children.

There is, in our judgment, no justification for the maintenance of a segregated school system. Given the history of our society, however, and the fact that the black population has been saddled with an inferior school system, there is room for honest differences of opinion about how the current situation can best be remedied. Ideally, all schools should be immediately desegregated—at every grade level. Practically, however, most schools are not equipped to cope with desegregation in this complete sense, and, when they are not, we suspect that it is the black child who is most likely to suffer under immediate and complete desegregation. To believe otherwise would be to deny our history in such matters. If someone is likely to get the "short end," the odds favor the minority child.

In retrospect, the Supreme Court probably would have been wiser in 1954 had it ordered the *immediate* implementation of a grade-a-year plan of desegregation (beginning with the first grade),[17] supplemented by a freedom-of-choice plan for all other grades. Indeed, although the hour seems quite late, this still may be the most desirable course of action to follow from the point of view of the black child. Some black children can compete successfully in a white school at any grade level, but far too many are ill prepared to switch at the upper grades from an inferior system to one whose academic standards are appreciably higher. To force poorly prepared children to make such a switch probably operates to their disadvantage, particularly when the resources of the schools are not

[17] Irwin Katz (1968, p. 266) reaches the following conclusion: "The foregoing material indicates that when grade-a-year plans of desegregation are adopted, it is obviously desirable from an educational standpoint to begin integration at the lowest grade and work upward. However, many southern school systems are on grade-a-year plans of reverse order, with integration starting in the twelfth grade and proceeding down."

increased to enable them to cope with the problems that such children present.[18]

Teachers' Expectations (The Self-Fulfilling Prophecy)

Many observers believe that a teacher's expectation of how a child will achieve in the classroom affects how he actually does perform (see Clark, 1965). This is sometimes called an example of the "self-fulfilling prophecy," that is, the predictor—in this case, the teacher—tends to obtain what he predicts by "arranging" the situation so that his prediction is validated. It is not implied that the predictor exerts his influence to this end deliberately; indeed, the argument usually is that he is unaware of what he is doing in this regard.

As Robert Rosenthal and Lenore Jacobson (1968a, pp. 219–253) have shown, the self-fulfilling prophecy may be applied to many contexts, including studies of animals. In the classroom it may be an important factor to consider in analyzing the behavior (both intellective and nonintellective) of any child, irrespective of his race, sex, social class, or other distinguishing characteristic. But it is obviously of special importance for the black child since our culture has conceptualized him as inferior intellectually. If teachers—be they black or white—accept this concept, they may, according to the self-fulfilling prophecy, obtain a lower scholastic performance than if they reject it. Furthermore, if this concept is accepted more widely and deeply among white teachers than among black, it may add another burden for the black child to carry as he moves into the desegregated classroom presided over by a white teacher.

That teachers' expectations do operate to the black child's disadvantage as far as his scholastic performance is concerned, however, has not been demonstrated satisfactorily; this is an hypothesis that needs to be tested by a series of carefully designed and conducted studies. Some guidelines in this regard can be found by scrutinizing an investigation reported recently by Robert Rosenthal and Lenore Jacobson (1968a, 1968b). Although the possession of a black skin was not an issue in this study, the researchers (1968a, p. 230) presented evidence to support ". . .

---

[18] One of our concerns is what desegregation at all grade levels does to the self-esteem of black children. As we shall show in the following chapter, there is evidence which *suggests* that black self-esteem may be damaged under such circumstances.

the hypothesis that, within a given classroom, those children from whom the teacher expected greater growth in intellectual competence would show such greater growth. . . ." This supposed finding caused a flurry of excitement in many quarters since it offered at least a partial nongenetic explanation for the low scholastic performance of disadvantaged children. It also suggested a quick and direct solution to a complex problem: raise teachers' expectations and their pupils' achievements will be significantly increased.

Unfortunately, as Richard E. Snow (1969) shows, the Rosenthal–Jacobson study had too many faults in its design and execution to permit us to accept its conclusions without deep reservations. This does not mean, however, that the hypothesis should be rejected. Instead, it should be tested by more carefully designed studies which give special attention to the validity of the hypothesis for black children. And, in our judgment, such studies should be built around academic achievement tests, not IQ tests.[19] It is vital that we know about this matter so that we can cope with it effectively as desegregation proceeds, if it indeed is a significant factor that differentially influences the black child in the classroom.

This brief discussion of the self-fulfilling prophecy should not lead the reader to conclude that it is applicable only to scholastic endeavors. As a matter of fact, it may be easier to demonstrate its validity in nonacademic settings as far as the black man is concerned. In many work situations, for example, it has been customary to expect a lesser performance from the black man, and he has been paid accordingly. And, in turn, there is informal evidence to suggest that the white man frequently has received what he has paid for when operating under this expectation. To expect more, pay more, and receive more has not been entertained as an alternative hypothesis in many work situations, even though it might have produced an increase in net profits.

Teachers' Views of Their Children

The Rosenthal–Jacobson study raises the question of how teachers do view their pupils with respect to their behavioral characteristics. In this

[19] Rosenthal and Jacobson obtained measures of intelligence, academic achievement, and nonintellective behavioral traits. In presenting their data, however, they emphasized changes in IQ, attempting to show that over the period of a school year children who were expected to show intellectual growth (this expectation was communicated to the teachers by the experimenters) gained, on the average, almost four more IQ points than children who were not expected to show such growth.

context, of course, our primary interest is in how black and white teachers compare in this regard. Do they tend to evaluate their pupils similarly, or are there significant differences in their judgments?

This question was investigated in the Millfield study during the years 1962 and 1964. In each of these years, every child of elementary school age was rated by his teacher on 22 behavior scales. In all, over 1,000 children were rated during each of the two years on the following personal characteristics:

1. Activity level
2. Emotional expressiveness
3. Dependency
4. Need for encouragement
5. Gregariousness
6. Achievement motivation
7. Social poise
8. Reaction to failure
9. Warmth
10. Cooperativeness
11. Effort expended on lessons
12. Emotional stability
13. Submissiveness
14. Suspiciousness
15. Tenacity
16. Anxiety level
17. Reaction to success
18. Cheerfulness
19. Aggressiveness
20. Attentiveness
21. Consistency
22. Teacher's liking of child

The data from the two years were combined and mean scores on each of the 22 traits were computed separately for the black and white children. The mean scores produced by this analysis are shown in Figure 12, separately for the two races.[20] Statistical analysis of the data confirmed what a visual inspection of Figure 12 suggests, namely, that the judgments of the white and black teachers were very similar. Nevertheless, there were some differences that cannot be overlooked. Thus, the white children were rated as being more emotionally expressive, less submissive, and less likeable (by their teachers) than the black children. The white children were also rated higher on their concern about the quality of their work and on their reaction to achievement or success experiences. In short, the black children were rated as being more passive and as showing less striving for achievement than their white counterparts.

Further analyses showed, however, that sex differences within *both* races were much greater than the racial differences just described. Also,

[20] In Figure 12, on some items socially desirable behavior is represented by peaks on the profile, on other items by valleys. See Baughman and Dahlstrom (1968) for greater detail.

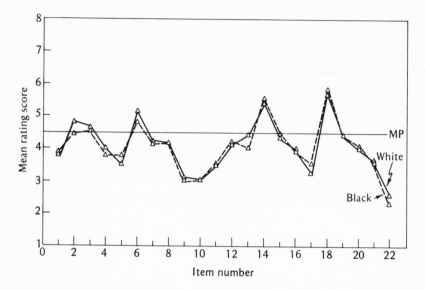

Fig. 12. Mean rating scores given by teachers to black and white children on 22 behavior scales (MP = midpoint of rating scale). (From Baughman & Dahlstrom, 1968.)

the sex differences among the black children were almost identical with those among the white children. Teachers of both races reported social, temperamental, and motivational differences between the two sexes that could almost always be said to favor the girls. Perhaps of critical importance is the fact that boys of both races evidenced lower achievement motivation than the girls.

Perhaps we should remind the reader that these data were collected under segregated conditions. We cannot be certain, of course, how similar the behavior profiles would appear in desegregated school systems.

Chapter 4/Self-Esteem

We turn now to the consideration of another quality that has loomed large in most psychological analyses of the black, namely, his *self-esteem.* By self-esteem we mean the regard or value that a person places on himself. Psychologists generally agree that individuals, whatever their color, vary with respect to the *amount* of self-esteem that they possess. In other words, self-esteem is usually considered in quantitative terms; one person, for example, may have *more* self-esteem than another.

We shall begin this section with a brief résumé of traditional thinking about the self-esteem of the black American. Then, because we consider this traditional view to be deficient in several important respects, we shall point out why a reformulation of thought in this domain is overdue. Finally, to buttress our position in this regard, we shall report on three recent empirical studies which have focused upon the self-esteem of black Americans.

The Traditional View

That the black American has been treated as an inferior human being needs no documentation here. The white majority needed to promote such a view, of course, to justify both slavery and the second-class citizenship to which the black was assigned following the abolition of slavery. Central to this view has been the idea that the black is inferior in the intellectual sense, but also emphasized has been the idea that the black is more primitive or "animal-like" in the way he expresses basic impulses such as sex and aggression.

Since an individual's self-concept is based upon his experiences and since American society has gone to great lengths to teach the black that he is inferior, it has commonly been accepted that the black has somehow internalized this prevailing valuation and made it his own. The result, according to this formulation, is that the black experiences a deficiency in self-esteem. Or, as Jean D. Grambs (1965, p. 15) concludes: "The self-esteem of the Negro is damaged by the overwhelming fact that the world he lives in says, 'White is right; black is bad.' "

What evidence is there to support conclusions similar to those reached by Grambs? Much of this evidence is in fact anecdotal, not unlike that advanced by C. F. Gibson, a black psychiatrist, who published a paper in 1931 with the title "Concerning Color." In this paper Gibson analyzes how black people respond to color and how it influences "their mental attitudes and personality makeups (p. 413)." To illustrate the negative valuation placed upon black, he cites a Negro church with doorways painted a light shade of tan. "If, upon entering the church, an individual was seen to be of a complexion darker than the doorway, membership in the church was denied him (p. 413)."

A second type of evidence may be described as clinical in nature. It is perhaps best exemplified by Abram Kardiner's and Lionel Ovesey's classic book, *The Mark of Oppression: Explorations in the Personality of the American Negro* (1951). These authors based their report on intensive psychoanalytic studies of 25 black Americans, and some of the material they present suggests diminished self-esteem in their patients linked to their color. For example, one mother, light in color, became quite distressed when she gave birth to a dark child and she refused to accept it as her own. More recently (1968), two black psychiatrists, W. F. Grier and P. M. Cobbs, have published a widely read book, *Black Rage*, which presents much additional clinical evidence that supports the hypothesis that black individuals struggle to cope with diminished supplies of self-esteem. In their words (1969 ed., p. 25): "Persisting to this day is an attitude, shared by black and white alike, that blacks are inferior."

A third type of evidence is more objective and quantitative than the anecdotal and clinical data. Although it has taken many forms, this research has usually attempted to identify the time at which children become aware of race (and their own racial membership) and the nature of their racial preferences. The work of Kenneth B. and Mamie P. Clark is probably cited most often in this regard, although a number of other researchers have made similar contributions (see, for example, Horowitz, 1939; Goodman, 1952; Landreth & Johnson, 1953). In one of the Clarks's studies (1947, pp. 169–178), for example, they asked 119 Northern and 134 Southern black children (ages 3–7, both male and female) to choose one of four dolls (two white, two black) in response to each of eight questions: Which is a nice doll? Which looks like a Negro child? Which looks like you? And so on.

Research of this type indicates that some children become aware of race as early as age three, and almost all children have such an awareness by age six or seven. When group data are considered, however, it is during the fourth year that the increase in racial awareness is most marked. There is no clear indication that either blacks or whites differ in the rate at which they develop such awareness. In studies like these, both black and white children give responses which indicate that they prefer a white skin to a black skin. For the black children, of course, this suggests that they have a negative evaluative attitude about a key component of their physical makeup.

It is clear, then, that there is a great deal of evidence suggesting that the black develops negative self-attitudes simply because of his color and the prevailing valuation that society has placed upon it. Although much of this evidence is not acceptable if rigorous scientific criteria are applied to it, nevertheless it cannot be ignored or dismissed until better evidence is advanced to replace it.

A Reconsideration of the Traditional View

Carefully gathered data which do not agree well with certain aspects of the traditional view of black self-esteem have in fact recently become available; they will be summarized in the following section. These data have forced us to rethink this problem, looking for ways in which the traditional analysis may be inadequate. Some of our thoughts in this regard will be presented here, before we turn to the empirical studies which prompted them.

1. Persistence of an Out-Dated Image?

What we have called the "traditional view" of black self-esteem continues to dominate contemporary thinking about this issue. This is illustrated, for example, by the key position paper delivered by Jean D. Grambs (1965) at a conference called to consider the Negro self-concept as it relates to education and citizenship. It is quite possible, however, that much of this thinking has become "dated" and no longer is an accurate representation of contemporary black self-attitudes, at least not those of black youth. This possibility was forcefully advanced by an unidentified black participant in the conference noted above during the discussion of Grambs' paper (see Kvaraceus, Gibson, Patterson, Seasholes, & Grambs, 1965, p. 43):

> It is interesting to note that all the major leaders among Negroes today tend to be quite Negroid in appearance. In fact, my black skin has a great value among Negroes today. I do remember a time when being as black as I am did not have much value, but today it is different.
>
> Who is indeed the New Negro we are talking about? As a matter of fact, as I read the position paper, it seemed to me that you were talking about the American Negro such as I was twenty years ago or ten years ago, or even three or four years ago. But now we have to consider that the Negro about whom we have concern is not the same kind of creature that was the object of research in the 1940's. The Negro of 1963 is certainly not the Negro of 1952 or even of 1959. In February, 1960, the sit-ins began. A whole new kind of way of living and a whole new concept of the Negro began, and reached larger masses and groups of Negroes.

At the very least, then, much of the research that continues to be cited in discussions of black self-esteem needs to be replicated before we accept it as valid for today's black. "Black is beautiful" may not be embraced by all blacks, but neither can we dismiss this thought as something akin to wishful thinking by those who do articulate it. Times have changed, and the black's view of himself may indeed be more positive than it was even a few years ago.

2. Did (Does) a Minority Group Internalize the Majority Group's View?

In reading and thinking about the issue at hand, we also began to realize that many "authorities" may have overestimated the extent to which blacks internalized the white's definition of them as inferior human beings. That some blacks have been so affected, there can be no doubt. On the other hand, the fact that so many blacks learned to *act* subservient or inferior in the presence of whites cannot be taken as conclusive evidence that they actually *felt* this way about themselves. Although the analogy is admittedly an imperfect one, this type of thinking would force us to conclude that the Jews have been similarly affected by how their oppressors have defined them. Perhaps they have been, but we know of no evidence that supports such a conclusion.

We are not asserting here that the self-esteem of the blacks was not sometimes damaged by the treatment he received at the hands of his oppressor who controlled most of the sources of power, but we are raising the possibility that the black resisted the white's definition of him more effectively than most observers have usually estimated. After all, the black was caught in a situation where he could see that most of his problems could be attributed to the repressive power of others; realistically, he did not have to look inward for deficiencies in his own self to explain his multitudinous difficulties. If this analysis is correct, then we should not be surprised to find that when the power structure began to change in the 1950's and 1960's there was a substantial reservoir of positive feelings about being black to draw upon.

The literature on the black has, we believe, given undue emphasis to his subservient behavior and roles. (We frequently forget that countless whites act in a similar fashion.) Too little attention has been devoted to blacks who evidenced pride and competence, even when they were not free. Moreover, we need to reconsider the power of any minority group to resist incorporating the definition of itself offered by an oppressive majority group, and this includes the black American minority.

3. Is the Black–White Distinction Quantitative?

Most discussions of black self-esteem either state explicitly or imply that the average black has *less* self-esteem than the average white. Research by our students (see pp. 48-55) causes us not only to doubt the validity of this conclusion *for contempory black youth*, but leads us to question whether it was ever true. Instead, we suggest that an alternate hypothesis should be given serious consideration; namely, that, in the quantitative sense, the supply of self-esteem is not, and has not been, less for the black than for the white.

It is clear, of course, that the life of the average black American continues to differ markedly from that of the average white American; there simply is no basis for argument about this. The hypothesis that we have advanced above, however, is based upon the belief that this difference in life pattern does not in fact produce a meaningful black–white gap in *level* of self-esteem. Blacks and whites may reach this level by different routes because of their different experiences, but they are not to be distinguished because one has *more* self-esteem than the other.

This hypothesis does not require us to reject the idea that the self-esteem of vast numbers of blacks is damaged, to use Grambs's terminology. Rather, it forces us to consider the possibility that the self-esteem of the average white is also significantly damaged by his experiences in the social structure of which he is a part. In this regard, we suspect that the black often overestimates the degree of self-satisfaction that resides in his white neighbor. Indeed, the very fact that the white man has found it necessary to push the black man down as inferior suggests the operation of a compensatory mechanism, the goal being to reassure the white of his own self-worth. If in fact he felt secure and adequate, such behavior would not be necessary. Furthermore, both blacks and whites seem to forget that material possessions and the possession of power do not automatically convert into feelings of self-esteem for those who hold them. One may have vast wealth and great power yet feel deeply inadequate; conversely, the most humble person may have genuine pride and dignity.

What this analysis suggests, of course, is that most discussions of black self-esteem fail to give adequate consideration to white self-esteem and how it may also be damaged within our social structure. While it undoubtedly is true that black self-esteem is frequently imparied, it does not necessarily follow that the black man is worse off in this regard than the white man. The white man, *for different reasons* and despite appearances to the contrary, may not develop more self-esteem than the black man.

4. How Is Self-Esteem Developed?

We have reached the point now where we must ask ourselves how self-esteem is developed. If the possession of material goods, power, and similar conditions do not automatically convert into feelings of self-worth, what factors are critical? Although we cannot explore this problem deeply here, we do want to touch upon several considerations which may be important as far as the black–white comparison is concerned.

There is general agreement that the antecedents of self-esteem are to be found in the childhood experiences of an individual. Furthermore, the child's family is usually regarded as the single most important determinant of how he comes to value himself, and, within the family, the influence of the parents (or parent substitutes) is viewed as having special significance. Stanley Coopersmith (1967), who has conducted an extensive inquiry into the antecedents of self-esteem, concludes that three components of parental behavior stand out as determinants of self-esteem (1968, p. 30):

The major factors that contribute to the formation of *high* self-esteem can be briefly described in terms of three conditions: *acceptance* of the child by his parents (or surrogates); clearly defined *limits* and values; and *respect* and latitude within the defined limits. In effect the parents are concerned and attentive, offer guidance and direction by structuring the world, and permit considerable freedom and individual expression so that initiative and communication are fostered.

Although Coopersmith's research involved white, middle-class boys and should be repeated with black children, there is no reason to believe that parental behavior is not also a critical determinant of black self-esteem. Furthermore, because, on the average, black family life is more disorganized than white family life (see pp. 77–78), we might expect that the types of parental behavior found by Coopersmith to be necessary for the development of positive self-regard would be encountered less frequently by black children. If this is true, shouldn't the level of self-esteem among black children be lower than that among white children? This, of course, is a conclusion that we have been arguing against and shall continue to do so.

We believe that the conclusion does not follow because children respond to parental behavior not in terms of its qualities measured along absolute scales but rather in a comparative or relativistic framework. More explicitly, a child perceives how he is treated in comparison with other children in his family—or to how other children in his circle are treated by their parents—and it is this concrete, comparative process that provides him with cues regarding his worth. If other children seem to be favored, for example, this signals to him that he must be less worthy than they. Compared to "parents in general" a particular set of parents may respond favorably to a child, but they may be even more positive in their behavior toward a second child in the family and thereby lay the basis for feelings of inadequacy in the first child. The child has no basis for evaluating the behavior of his parents against the general average, but he can judge the responses he receives against those secured by his siblings and members of his peer group. In a similar way, he can compare how he is treated by his teachers and other significant persons in his world with how other children are treated by the same individuals. This comparative process, we believe, is central to the concept that a child develops of himself.

It is also important to emphasize another point, namely, that the typical black child—whether urban or rural—spends his formative years in essentially a black world. The black community provides him with his frame of reference, and it is within the black community that the comparative process that we described above functions. Thus, the critical consideration in regard to the generation of self-esteem is that the black child compares himself with other black children, not with white children. His evaluative framework is provided by the black community and not by the larger community in which his group is actually a subculture. The pervasiveness of this orientation of black children was indicated by structured interviews conducted by black interviewers with adolescent blacks in the rural South (see Baughman & Dahlstrom, 1968). In answering questions about themselves, their families, their schools, and so on, it was clear that the black children consistently responded by comparing themselves to other black children, or their families to other black families, or their schools to other black schools. The fact that the community contained white families and white institutions did not seem to enter into establishing the framework within which they evaluated themselves and their institutions. This suggests, of course, that the critical factor for the black child—as far as his self-esteem is concerned—revolves around how he perceives himself treated within the black community compared to how other black children are treated in the same community. As long as his world remains overwhelmingly black, the white child's situation is largely irrelevant as far as the black child's self-concept is concerned.

As the black child grows older, however, it becomes increasingly difficult for him to maintain such a completely black orientation. For the urban child this time usually comes earlier than it does for the rural child, and for black children in general it probably comes sooner now than it did even a few years ago. Nevertheless, it continues to be true that this inevitable confrontation with the white world (in any really meaningful sense) occurs for most black children *after the foundation of their self-esteem has been established by their experiences within the black community.*

When the black child's world begins to enlarge, and especially when he is thrown into interactions with whites, the self-esteem that he has generated in a basically black context can be threatened. In some competitive contexts, however, his experiences with whites give him no basis for revising his self-concept to a more negative form; athletic competition is certainly a prime example of this. In other contexts—the desegregated classroom, for example—he is much more severely pressed and runs the risk of losing self-esteem. This, incidentally, is one reason why massive school desegregation at all grade levels poses such a difficult problem for the black child (especially the older one) and why it might have been advantageous to him if the Supreme Court in 1954 had ordered the immediate implementation of a grade-a-year plan (see earlier discussion, pp. 31–33).

When the black child discovers that he does not measure up well in interactions with whites, two psychological paths are open to him. He can interpret his experiences as evidence that he is less adequate than he had been led to believe (thus suffering a loss in self-esteem), or he can blame the "system" for having discriminated against him by providing him with inferior preparatory experiences (thus protecting his self-esteem). In other words, he has a choice between looking inward and finding the insufficiency there, or looking outward and finding the inadequacy there.[21] Today's black youth, we believe, are much more likely to follow the second path than the first, and, of course, it is not difficult for them to find an ample supply of evidence that the "system" has discriminated against them. Furthermore, they are encouraged and supported in this interpretation by many influential voices, both black and white.

[21] In "looking outward," he may, of course, challenge the "relevance" of white, middle-class standards.

The analysis that we have presented leads to a conclusion that may startle some readers: *for some individuals, being black actually is advantageous as far as self-esteem is concerned.* This is true because the discrimination that blacks have endured enables a black man to point "out there" to explain his frustrations, failures, and so on, rather than to deficiencies in his own self. The white man, clearly, cannot protect his self-esteem in the same manner. This may be why some whites are so upset when they see a black man who, by white standards, has achieved a level of success beyond their own. Seldom can they say, "He's achieved that just because he's black," whereas the unsuccessful black man frequently has at least some basis for reaching a comparable conclusion about many relatively successful white men. He does not have to accept their success as a true measure of his inadequacy.[22]

There is, of course, a real danger in this situation for the black man, especially now that many of the barriers to his progress are beginning to crumble. The danger is that he will fail to see how he may improve himself to take advantage of new opportunities, preferring instead to rather passively accept his "fate" as a product of a discriminating system. Discrimination will continue, of course, but today's scene is also speckled with instances of reverse discrimination, or situations where it is actually advantageous to be black. To mine these opportunities productively, the black man must honestly analyze his inner resources and seek opportunities to develop them; he must resist the temptation to protect his self-esteem from failure experiences by concluding in advance that the "system" dooms him to second-class roles.

Three Empirical Studies

As we noted earlier, much of the traditional thinking about black self-esteem has been based upon rather casual observations of black behavior, and the validity of the inferences that have been drawn therefrom is certainly questionable. Furthermore, the incidence of comparable behavior in the white population has usually been neglected. It is of particular interest, therefore, to consider the results of three recent empirical studies which directly asked groups of black and white children to make self-judgments. What do these investigations tell us about the comparative levels of self-esteem in black and white children?

---

[22] Increasingly, however, some whites are charging that blacks are receiving favoritism in special programs aimed at assisting the disadvantaged.

1. McDonald and Gynther

In 1965, Robert L. McDonald and Malcolm D. Gynther published the results of a study that bears upon the question just posed. Their data were collected in 1961 and 1962 in a southern urban area; the subjects were 261 black high school seniors (151 female, 110 male) and 211 white high school seniors (114 female, 97 male). The black subjects were graduating seniors of the city's only black high school, while the white subjects were graduating seniors of three of the seven white high schools. (The white schools were selected so as to represent different social classes and cultural settings.) Ages of the subjects ranged from 16 to 19.

School counselors (who were of the same race as their subjects) administered the Interpersonal Check List (ICL) to the above students in special group testing sessions. According to McDonald and Gynther (1965, p. 86), the ICL "... consists of 128 adjectives and phrases (for example, forceful, usually gives in, considerate, sarcastic) with 16 items for each of eight different kinds of interpersonal behavior." (Although the ICL purports to measure 8 dimensions of behavior, Dominance and Love are the primary dimensions tapped by this test; see below.) Each subject rated each item twice, first to describe his self and second to describe the person that he would ideally like to be (that is, his self-ideal). From these ratings, four scores were computed: Dominance (Self), Dominance (Ideal), Love (Self), and Love (Ideal). The Dominance score "... is a measure of assertive, aggressive, leadership qualities" while the Love score "... is a measure of friendly, warm, cooperative characteristics (1965, p. 85)." (The two ideal scores, of course, define how the subjects would like to be with respect to Dominance and Love characteristics.)

Results for the two Dominance scores are plotted in Figure 13, separately for the two races. As shown there, the mean Dominance (Self) score for the black students is higher than that of the white students, but the mean Dominance (Ideal) score of the blacks is comparatively low. The same pattern characterizes the two Love scores (figure not shown). For both characteristics, then, the black students are closer to their ideals than the white students are to theirs.[23]

The discrepancy between self and self-ideal is frequently used in psychological research as a measure of self-esteem, that is, the greater the

___

[23] Statistically, McDonald and Gynther (1965, p. 87) show that "... there is much less discrepancy between self- and ideal-self-descriptions of the Negro students than the white students...." ($P < .001$ for both Dominance and Love.)

48   4. Self-Esteem

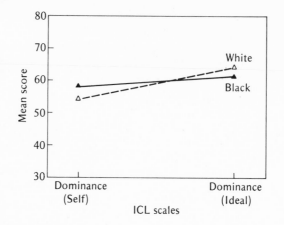

Fig. 13. Mean Dominance scores (Self and Self-Ideal) for black and white high school seniors. (Based upon data from McDonald & Gynther, 1965.)

discrepancy between self and self-ideal the lower the individual's self-esteem is inferred to be. If this is a justifiable inference, the McDonald–Gynther data lead us to conclude that the self-esteem of their black subjects is *higher*, on the average, than that of their white subjects. Although they do not attempt to explain their findings, McDonald and Gynther do point out that "... the results involving race would seem contrary to lay expectations. . . . (p. 87)." We would go even further and conclude that the results are contrary to what one would predict based upon much of what has been written about black self-esteem by professionals.

2. *Wendland*

A second study of interest to us was conducted by Marilyn M. Wendland in 1967. All of her subjects were in the eighth grade and ranged in age from 13 to 17 (mean age was approximately 14). The total sample of 685 children was composed of 176 white boys, 161 white girls, 151 black boys, and 197 black girls.

Wendland drew her subjects from four different types of residential areas in central North Carolina: one rural area, one village, two small towns (populations approximately 15,000), and one city (population about 90,000). With a few exceptions, all of the children came from either lower or lower-middle class families. The black children were attending all-black schools and the white children were enrolled in essentially all-white schools, although there was token integration in some of the white schools.[24] Data were gathered from these children in small group sessions conducted by a female examiner of the same race as the subjects.[25]

Wendland's primary test instrument was the Tennessee Self Concept Scale (TSCS) which was administered to each of the 685 subjects. According to Wendland (1967, p. 38), this test "... consists of 100 short sentences that a subject rates on a five-point continuum from completely true to completely false as they pertain to himself." Examples of the type of statement contained in the TSCS are "I am a decent sort of person" and "I like my looks just the way they are."

Wendland also had her subjects respond to a scale designed to measure feelings of *estrangement* and to a second scale which attempts to determine the degree of one's *cynicism* toward his environment.[26] In addition, each subject filled out a questionnaire to provide personal information about himself and his family. Special precautions were taken (see Wendland, 1967) to ensure that limitations in a child's reading ability did not invalidate his responses to any of the three scales or the questionnaire.

Many scores can be derived from the TSCS (see Fitts, 1965), but our primary interest here is in what is called the Total Positive Score, or, simply, *P*. This score, according to Wendland (1967, p. 38), "Reflects the overall level of self-esteem. Persons with high scores tend to like themselves, feel that they are persons of value and worth, and act accordingly. People with low scores are doubtful about their own worth; see themselves as undesirable; often feel anxious, depressed, and unhappy; and have little confidence in themselves."

The analysis of Wendland's data revealed that the mean self-esteem score (that is, *P* score) of the black children significantly *exceeded* that of the white children. Also, within both races, girls scored higher than boys. Finally, children living in the country secured, on the average, higher scores than children living in the other three types of residential areas. All of these findings are depicted in Figure 14. (In this figure, the scores of

---

[24] The few black children in white schools were not included in Wendland's study.

[25] There was one exception; circumstances made it necessary for a white examiner to test one black group.

[26] These two scales were developed by R. H. Harrison and E. H. Kass (1967) using items from the Minnesota Multiphasic Personality Inventory.

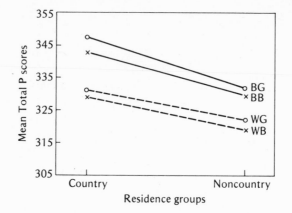

Fig. 14. Mean Total *P* scores for black and white eighth-graders according to sex and residential area. (Based upon data from Wendland, 1967.)

village, town, and city children have been combined to form a "noncountry" group since there were no significant differences in the scores of these children associated with their residential area.)

Figure 15 shows the mean Estrangement and Cynicism scores secured by the children of both races. These results are very interesting for they indicate that the black children feel more alienated or estranged from others in their environment than the white children, but, simultaneously, as reflected in the Cynicism scores, they are, compared to the white children, much more inclined to find fault with others than with themselves. This suggests, of course, a marked tendency among black children to account for their inner unrest by finding fault with their environment rather than by seeing deficiencies in themselves.[27]

In reflecting upon her findings, Wendland comments as follows (1967, pp. 106–108):

> Contrary to descriptions in much of the literature, the Negro adolescents in this study, regardless of area of residence, do not present a picture of self-devaluation and negative self-esteem in comparison with their white peers. The question remains as to how, in the face of inferior caste status, these adolescents are able to

[27] In Wendland's data, Estrangement and Cynicism scores show a positive correlation of .61.

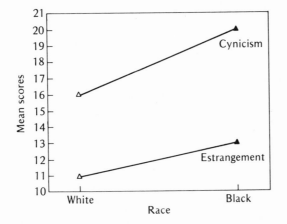

Fig. 15. Mean Cynicism and Estrangement scores for white and black eighth-graders. (Based upon data from Wendland, 1967.)

maintain a positive image of themselves. One suggestive possibility emerges from the analysis of the MMPI Cynicism scale scores. While they obtained higher self-concept scores, the Negro group also scored significantly higher on the Cynicism scale, reflecting an orientation of mistrust and unfavorable attitudes toward other people. It is thus suggested that the Negro adolescent may react to the dis-esteem in which he is held by interpreting this as an expression of pathology in the discriminator rather than an inadequacy in himself. . . .

Thus, maintenance of positive self-esteem is coupled with a cynical orientation toward others and, in consequence, a feeling of isolation from others. In part, then, the results of this study suggest that conceptualizations of the Negro found in the older literature may represent unfounded stereotypes and generalizations. It also seems likely, however, that the discrepancy reflects some recent basic changes in Negro self-attitudes. Given the changes in Negro status in the last decade, it is obvious that positive self-feelings have become more possible. Additionally, the adaptive value of assuming a self-derogatory stance in confrontations with white society is less evident. In Negro sub-groups such as the Black Power movement such self-derogation is, moreover, clearly maladaptive. In reconciling the results of the present study with older literature, it is thus suggested that not only is a basic change in Negro self-evaluation emerging, but also that the instrumental value of *claiming* self-devaluation no longer serves its historical purpose.

3. *Bridgette*

The third set of data that we shall refer to were *collected* by Richard E. Bridgette in 1968. His subjects were eleventh-graders who lived in both the village and country areas of North Carolina from which Wendland drew her sample The average age of Bridgette's subjects was slightly under 17, or approximately three years older than those of Wendland.

Bridgette obtained various types of information from his subjects in order to study both the antecedents and consequences of self-esteem. We cannot summarize all of his findings here; instead, we shall focus upon the self-esteem measure as it reflects on the question of racial differences. Bridgette measured the self-esteem of his eleventh-graders by administering Coopersmith's Self-Esteem Inventory (SEI) to them. The SEI (see Coopersmith, 1967) consists of 50 items which the subject must check as being either like or unlike him (Example: "I'm proud of my school work.") plus eight items (called the Lie scale and also answered as either "Like Me" or "Unlike Me") which attempt to measure the respondent's defensiveness. That is, in answering the SEI, does the subject "stretch the truth" to give an overly positive picture of himself or does he perhaps lean in the opposite direction in giving his answers?

Bridgette's subjects were attending a high school that had been desegregated about three months before the SEI was administered to them. They took this inventory in their mixed classes; one black and one white male examiner were randomly assigned to these classes for data gathering purposes.[28] In all, Self-Esteem scores were secured for 252 subjects (39 black males, 53 black females, 78 white males, and 82 white females).

The mean Self-Esteem scores for the four race–sex groups are shown in Figure 16. Of primary interest is the fact that the white children of both sexes scored higher than their black counterparts. This difference is opposite to that reported by Wendland at a younger age level using a different test instrument. Also, the direction of the sex difference reported

[28]The data analysis showed that the race of the examiner did not have a significant influence on the Self-Esteem scores.

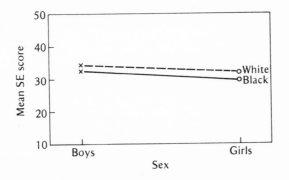

Fig. 16. Mean Self-Esteem (SE) scores for white and black eleventh-graders according to sex of subjects. (Based upon data from Bridgette, 1970.)

by Bridgette is opposite to that found by Wendland (compare Figures 14 and 16).

Although the racial difference obtained by Bridgette is not large, it cannot be ignored. It may be, of course, that the difference between Wendland's findings and Bridgette's is due to their use of different measuring instruments. Or it may be due to the age differential between the subjects in the two studies. However, the results of the McDonald–Gynther study (see above) would argue against age being the critical factor since subjects in that study were slightly older than Bridgette's. Nevertheless, it is clear that we badly need longitudinal studies of self-esteem in which various measures of self-esteem are used.

There is a situational factor in Bridgette's study which was not present in the two previously summarized investigations and we should give it some consideration in interpreting Bridgette's results. Reference here is to the fact that his data were collected *after* the students had been attending school under desegregated conditions. Moreover, the desegregation had not gone smoothly—there had been overt conflict and several black students had been either suspended or expelled. These difficulties occurred in a school situation in which whites outnumbered blacks by about two to one and in a community which had used every available means to resist desegregation.

In this desegregated school it was clear that the average black student was not able to compete on equal terms with the average white student. For the first time many black students were forced to realize that academically they were not as well prepared as the white students.

Although some of the students undoubtedly blamed the racist system for having given them inferior preparation, it is also likely that others were forced into reappraisals of themselves with consequent loss in self-esteem.[29] If this latter process did indeed occur, it could account for the differences between Wendland's and Bridgette's findings.

It is relevant in this regard to note that Bridgette had a group IQ test (the Otis Quick Scoring Mental Ability Test—Form Gamma) administered to each of his subjects. On this test the mean IQ of the black children was 87, or 20 points below that of the white children. Although IQ and Self-Esteem scores were not highly correlated (r = .19 over all subjects), these two measures were more highly correlated for the black children than for the white children. Moreover, when the effect due to IQ was removed by statistical procedures, *the racial difference in self-esteem scores was no longer significant.* Indirectly this suggests, we believe, that the black children may have been sensitive to the fact that they were functioning at a lower average ability level than their white classmates and that they suffered a loss in self-esteem as a consequence. Hopefully, more direct evidence bearing on this interpretation can be generated by future research.

Finally, let us note that the correlation between Lie scores (see above) and Self-Esteem scores was higher for the white children than for the black children, but that the Lie scores were higher for the blacks than for the whites. As Bridgette shows in the analysis of his data, however, these findings do not substantially alter the interpretation of the results that we have already reported.

Parental Behavior and Self-Esteem. Earlier we observed that "Although Coopersmith's research involved white, middle-class boys and should be repeated with black children, there is no reason to believe that parental behavior is not also a critical determinant of black self-esteem." Another part of Bridgette's work compels us to reconsider this proposition.

Each child in Bridgette's study was asked to make judgments about 13 components of his parents' behavior (Example: Who usually punishes you?—Mother—Father—Both—Neither). Included in these 13 evaluations were those aspects of parental behavior which Coopersmith had found to be related to the self-esteem of his white, middle-class boys. Bridgette's

[29] This is why, as we commented in our discussion of scholastic performance, the black child may have to pay a significant emotional price for immediate desegregation at the upper grade levels.

data show that 8 of the 13 evaluations do relate significantly to the Self-Esteem scores of his white subjects, but there is not even one significant relationship in the data for the black subjects. This does not indicate that parental behavior is not a significant determinant of black self-esteem, but it does warn us to be extremely cautious in transferring findings from white to black populations. What seems obvious, of course, is that we must always study black as well as white samples if we wish to achieve valid generalizations with regard to such problems. Indeed, even though Bridgette's study does not prove this, it may turn out that socialization practices in the typical black family are enough different from those in the typical white family that parental behavior is not as critical a determinant of black self-esteem as it is of white self-esteem. In any event, it is clear that we need more empirical studies of how both black and white children develop self-esteem.

A Final Comment

We rather suspect that as behavioral scientists we know somewhat less about the generation of self-esteem than we would like to believe. Sullivan, Mead, Erikson, and others are cited so often that we have come to accept their explanations of the origin of self-esteem not as hypotheses but as established facts. With respect to the black man, we have too readily assumed an isomorphic relationship between his disadvantaged position and the regard that he holds for himself. Through comparative studies of an empirical nature perhaps we can achieve a more valid picture of both the black man and the white man, as well as a more accurate understanding of the processes which are critical in determining how each comes to conceive of his own self.

The data that we have presented—particularly that of Wendland—also suggest that blacks may pay a high price in other sectors of their personality in order to protect a reasonably strong sense of self-esteem. To have high self-esteem while also maintaining a cynical attitude towards others (blacks as well as whites) and feeling estranged from others can hardly be viewed as desirable as would be a comparable level of self-esteem maintained in a context containing less cynicism and fewer feelings of estrangement.

Chapter 5/Rage and Aggression

... all blacks are angry. White Americans seem not to recognize it. They seem to think that all the trouble is caused by only a few "extremists."

... the emerging rage now threatens to shatter this nation. ...

... many whites are haunted by a vision of being oppressed, exposed to the whims of a powerful cruel black man. ... No one can doubt that white America is afraid.

Even today, the black man cannot become too aggressive without hazard to himself.

Today black boys are admonished not to be a "bad nigger." No description need be offered; every black child knows what is meant. They are angry and hostile. They strike fear into everyone with their uncompromising rejection of restraint or inhibition. ... every black man harbors a potential bad nigger inside him.

... there can be no doubt of the universality of black rage.

The above quotes, all drawn from the popular *Black Rage* (1968) written by two black psychiatrists, William H. Grier and Price M. Cobbs, serve well as an introduction to the topic that we shall discuss briefly in this section, rage and aggression.

Only the insensitive white American can be surprised to hear that "all blacks are angry." To believe otherwise given the black's history in America surely is to reveal a psychological obtuseness of the greatest proportions. Yet the myth of the "happy nigger" continues to persist in some quarters, even at a time when the riots in Watts, Detroit, and Newark have struck deep fears in so many Americans, both white and black.

The truth of the matter is that relatively few whites have been interested in discerning and understanding the true feelings of that one-tenth of the population who are called blacks. It has contributed to the security and prosperity of the whites to believe that blacks were happy and contented with their lot in life, and countless whites have so believed. But when the *overt behavior* of the blacks begins to threaten the security and possessions of the whites, the latter are forced to reexamine some of their simplistic and self-serving assumptions about the former.

An angry person will, we believe, always betray the nature of his inner feelings in some way. Frequently, however, this manifestation will be quite subtle or indirect; consequently it is easy for these feelings to go unrecognized by the person who, for psychological reasons of his own, does not want to see them. Historically, of course, black Americans have always been in a position where it was extremely dangerous for them to express their anger by means of direct aggression against their white oppressors. And, although restrictions in this regard in contemporary society may be less than they have been in the past, it would be a gross distortion to pretend that they no longer exist. Economic reprisals against the "uppity nigger" are still quite common, for example, and the Black Panther believes that it may not take much provocation—if any at all—for certain policemen to eliminate him as a threat.

Channeling Black Aggression (Hortense Powdermaker)

More than 25 years ago, Hortense Powdermaker, an anthropologist, published a paper in which she described various ways in which black Americans channel their aggression.[30] Powdermaker's analysis is useful in organizing our thinking about this matter, especially since it helps us to point up some of the changes in the expression of black aggression that

---

[30] Let us be clear that the mechanisms which are about to be described are used by people of all colors; as Grier and Cobbs emphasize (1969, p.129), the *experiences* of black Americans are unique, not the *principles* or processes of psychological functioning.

have occurred during the past quarter of a century. The emphasis in Powdermaker's paper, of course, is upon the aggressive impulses of blacks which are aroused in their contacts with whites.

First, it is obvious that the black who is angered by the white may attack the source of his upset. Historically, however, this has been a channel that generally has been denied the black. Even with just cause, the black could mount an attack against the white only at extreme peril; almost certainly the white would counterattack backed up by the power of the broader white community. This fear of counteraggression continues to be pervasive in today's black community, and realistically so. Yet there are cracks in the dam and militant blacks are very visible, creating a conscious fear in the white community that was absent only a few years ago. And while it is true that the vast majority of blacks are not personally militant, there is also evidence that they tend to identify with and gain psychological strength from the relatively few blacks who do attack "Whitey" directly.

Instead of attacking the true object of his anger, however, the black may find a substitute object to act out against; usually this is another black who poses less of a threat in terms of counteraggression. The black man who has been degraded by his white employer, for example, may act in a cruel and inhuman way to his spouse and children. Or he may manifest a very "short fuse" when a conflict develops with another black man. Indeed, this capacity for displacement may be one of the reasons why the homicide rate for "blacks against blacks" is so high compared to that for "blacks against whites" (see Pettigrew, 1964).

Another possibility open to the black is to try to remain unaffected by the interracial situation, that is, not to respond to it at all. This, of course, is extremely difficult for the black (if not impossible) at some level within himself if he has contacts with whites or recognizes that in some way his behavior is circumscribed by white controls. Even if the black never ventures forth from the depths of the ghetto or if he isolates himself in all-black communities such as Mound Bayou, Mississippi or Boley, Oklahoma, the spectre of the white man is ever present. Nevertheless, back-to-Africa movements and programs calling for the establishment of a black nation within the United States continue to appeal to some blacks, essentially, we believe, because they seem to promise freedom from white provocation that has not been handled adequately by other means.

Another strategy available to the black is that of attempting to discharge some of his interracial hostility through wit or humor; laugh in order not to cry or die. In general, of course, whites know little about such humor since it is expressed only among blacks. Two white psychiatrists practicing in the South, however, were able, using black observers, to collect samples of jokes told by blacks to blacks (see Prange & Vitols, 1963). Their data do indeed show that a "striking number" (actually, 72%) of the jokes collected referred to race relations. Momentarily, of course, telling such stories must serve a useful psychological function for their tellers, yet it is equally obvious that this channel can serve as little more than a diversion and is not a long-term solution for the black's aggression.

A fifth adaptation employed by some blacks may be described as "identifying with the oppressor." Today this solution to the problem of aggression is probably less common than it was in the past simply because the black community has grown increasingly intolerant of it. During slavery, however, some blacks identified with the powerful families whom they served and, in some instances, were even more aggressive toward other blacks than their white masters. More recently, some blacks have identified with their white employers, especially when the latter have had great power or prestige. It is as if the black says to himself, "I am part of this powerful white family, therefore I cannot possibly be hostile to it or what it is part of." But, of course, he deludes himself.

The last pattern of adaptation described by Powdermaker is the one that she emphasizes the most, and it is an extremely familiar one. It is a pattern of behavior which has much in common with the "identification with the oppressor" syndrome just described, and it is one especially valued by whites. When a black learns to behave in this way, he is referred to as a "good nigger." Grier and Cobbs describe him this way (1969, pp. 55–56):

Granting the limitations of stereotypes, we should nevertheless like to sketch a paradigmatic black man. His characteristics seem so connected to employment that we call it "the postal-clerk syndrome." This man is always described as "nice" by white people. In whatever integrated setting he works, he is the standard against whom other blacks are measured. "If they were all only like him, everything would be so much better." He is passive, nonassertive, and nonaggressive. He has made a virture of identification with the aggressor, and he has adopted an ingratiating and compliant manner. In public his thoughts and feelings are consciously shaped in the direction he thinks white people want them to be. The pattern begins in childhood when the mother may actually say: "You must be this way because this is the only way you will get along with Mr. Charlie."

This man renounces gratifications that are available to others. He assumes a deferential mask. He is always submissive. He must figure out "the man" but keep "the man" from deciphering him. He is prevalent in the middle and upper-middle classes, but is found throughout the social structure. The more closely allied to the white man, the more complete the picture becomes. He is a direct lineal descendant of the "house nigger" who was designed to identify totally with the white master. The danger he poses to himself and others is great, but only the surface of passivity and compliance is visible. The storm below is hidden.

At the risk of oversimplification, let us suggest that white America fears this storm because it may replace the Postal Clerk with the Black Panther. But black America is also afraid; while blacks applaud (many secretly) a few Black Panthers, they are fearful of the counteraggression that might be unleashed if Black Panthers become too numerous

Is the Black More Aggressive than the White?

Vast numbers of whites continue to believe that the black is *innately* more aggressive than the white even though there is no scientific evidence to support such a belief. Some blacks have adopted a similar belief and use it to justify their child-training practices aimed at developing the postal-clerk syndrome described above. This is rather ironic, of course, when one stops to realize how much the black has been victimized by white aggression.

Why do so many whites see blacks as hyperaggressive? There is, obviously, no single answer to such a question, but three factors must be emphasized. First, whites have some information about the comparatively high incidence of extreme acts of aggression within the black American community, such as knifings, homicides, and so on. This leads them then to the quite unjustified conclusion that such aggression is somehow linked to the genetic makeup of the black rather than to his life experiences.

Other data which the ordinary white is not aware of show, of course, that blacks are capable of living harmoniously in social groups without the high incidence of aggression that is present in many parts of the United States. Mound Bayou, Mississippi (see p. 58), for example, went twenty years without one murder, while, contrary to the common stereotype of the primitive African, "Seventy-one percent of the 41 tribal groups studied by Bohannan and his associates [in East Africa] had lower homicide rates than the whites of either South Carolina or Texas in 1949–1951 (Pettigrew, 1964, pp. 143–144)."

A second factor contributing to the white's belief about the black's aggression is the white's realization that treatment of the black has been such that the black *should* respond aggressively even if he does not. This *identification* with the black need not be conscious, of course; nevertheless, many whites do recognize that if they were exploited the way the blacks are, they would lash out aggressively. As a result they perceive the black as being "loaded" with aggression and do all they can to see that his aggression is not expressed.

Also contributing to this aspect of the white's stereotype of the black is the process of *projection.* That is, instead of recognizing the hostile impulses that are a part of his own makeup, the white projects them onto the black and sees the latter as being more aggressive than he really is. "I'm not hostile, it's the black who is hostile." By such a process the white can simultaneously protect his self-image while taking what he rationalizes as counteraggressive actions against a hostile foe bent on his destruction.

But why, we must ask ourselves, do many blacks also view blacks as hyperaggressive? Again, there is no single answer to this question. Like whites, however, blacks may inappropriately generalize from their direct experiences with violence in the black American community and lack knowledge about the nonviolent behavior of blacks in other social settings. Equally important, however, most blacks probably recognize at some level within themselves the validity of the Grier–Cobbs observation (see p. 56) that "all blacks are angry." This means, of course, that the potential for aggression is ever present in themselves and their black brothers, and they know it. Thus, their conception of the black is deeply affected not just by what he does, but also by what they sense his potential to be.

Two Empirical Studies

It is clear that aggression may take many different forms. It is also true that the situational context will have a great deal of influence on whether or not a person will act aggressively. Therefore we should not be surprised to learn that psychologists have had limited success in devising means for measuring a general factor of aggressiveness in individuals. Indeed, our conclusion about a person's (or group's) level of aggression must always keep in mind the method of measurement, since different measuring procedures may produce different results. In this regard, it may be instructive to consider two empirical studies which attempted to compare black and white children on aggression.

1. Hammer

In 1953 E. F. Hammer published data gathered from elementary schoolchildren living in what he described as a "semi-rural, semi-urban" locale in Virginia. Four hundred children (148 black, 252 white) were asked to produce three drawings: a house, a tree, and a person. Independently, then, six clinicians evaluated each child's set of drawings in terms of how much aggression they contained: none (score 0), mild (score 1), or severe (score 2). These ratings were made without the clinicians knowing the racial identity of the persons whose drawings they were evaluating.

TABLE II

Mean Aggression Scores of Black and White Children by Grade Level [a]

	Race	
Grade	White	Black
1	.19	.84
2	.19	.88
3	.38	.75
4	.17	.82
5	.27	.81
6	.44	1.18
7	.47	.58
8	.36	.73
Overall Mean	.31	.82

[a]Based upon data from Hammer (1953). Drawings not containing aggression were scored 0, those containing mild aggression were scored 1, and those containing severe aggression were scored 2.

Analysis of Hammer's data showed that the mean aggression score of the black children was significantly higher than that of the white children. Furthermore, the scores of the black children were higher at each of the eight grade levels (see Table II). Do these findings indicate, however, that the average black child in Hammer's study is more aggressive than the average white child? Not necessarily, although, at the same time, neither can we rule out this possibility. Another possible interpretation is that the average black child perceives more aggression in his environment than the average white child and shows us this perception in his drawings. This second interpretation would be in essential agreement with findings reported by Paul H. Mussen (also in 1953) based upon stories told by both black and white boys to a series of 13 pictures: Mussen's black subjects gave indications of perceiving more hostility in their environments than his white subjects. Returning to Hammer's study, a third interpretation must be considered: his black subjects may be more aggressive than his white subjects *and* they may also perceive more aggression in the environment. Among these several possibilities, we must remain in doubt.

2. *Baughman and Dahlstrom*

As part of the Baughman—Dahlstrom study of rural children in central North Carolina, each of 480 children told 12 stories to pictures specially drawn to be free of racial bias. The children were divided equally with respect to race and sex at four age levels—7, 9, 11, and 13. Each child told his stories to a female examiner of his own race.

The stories gathered in this way were scored for 34 variables without the scorer having knowledge of the storyteller's race. Nine of these variables pertained to different forms of aggression that might be found in such stories (physical punishment, antisocial acts, verbal aggression, and so on). In addition, a tenth score attempted to summarize the total aggressive content of each story.

After intellective and verbal productivity differences between the subjects had been taken into account, analysis of the ten aggression scores revealed no significant differences in them that could be attributed to the racial identities of the subjects. However, the black children did attribute more unpleasant feelings—especially worry and anxiety—to the characters in their stories than the white children. Also, they made many more references to the basic necessities for living (food, clothing, shelter, and money) than was true for the white children.

These data, then, do not agree with those of Hammer which are summarized in Table II, p. 62. Perhaps it is the mode of evaluation that produces the difference, or the locale, or the 15-year discrepancy in time between the two studies; we simply cannot be certain why there is a difference between the results of the two studies. The heightened anxiety level of the characters in the stories told by the black children in the Baughman–Dahlstrom study along with their greater concern about the basic necessities of living, however, would agree with the earlier suggestion made with reference to both the Hammer and Mussen studies, that is, that *black children perceive their environments as more threatening than do white children.*

A Final Comment

While there is no evidence of innate differences in aggressive tendencies linked to racial membership, it is clear that socialization practices often have been directed toward the inhibition of aggression so as to produce the postal-clerk syndrome. Whites have had a vested interest in this process since it has enabled them to exploit the black, while blacks have supported it because their very survival has seemed to depend upon it. The result has been that black aggression in its most severe forms has been directed primarily against fellow blacks; there has been aggression against whites, of course, but usually this has been more subtle or indirect.

The contemporary black leadership recognizes that blacks must become more assertive, even aggressive, in their interracial behavior if they hope to achieve equal status in American society and fair access to its benefits. While the black masses may applaud the militant pronouncements of their leaders, however, it is extremely difficult for them to overthrow generations of tradition and actually act more assertively in interracial situations. This is particularly true because such behavior threatens a white majority that is capable of counteraggression. The black problem, therefore, almost defies solution—unless powerful forces in the white community (such as the legal establishment) rally to the support of blacks. Blacks must become more assertive and shed the postal-clerk syndrome; yet they must also skillfully manipulate forces so as to prevent counteraggression that could destroy the progress that has been made. This is truly a most difficult challenge.

Chapter 6/Psychopathology

Now we shall turn to a brief examination of deviant behavior among blacks. After considering data reflecting on the incidence of such behavior among blacks as compared to whites, problems encountered in interpreting the significance of these data will be outlined. This will bring us face to face with the question of whether there is a "Black Norm" that is separate from a "White Norm" which must be invoked when making judgments about the normality or abnormality of black behavior. Finally, a few of the special problems affecting the delivery of treatment services to the emotionally disturbed black will be discussed.

The Incidence[31] of Behavioral Disturbances among Blacks

As an overall generalization, data from a variety of sources support the statement that many pathological forms of behavior are relatively more common among blacks than among whites. With respect to some specific

[31] Pettigrew (1964, pp. 73-74) makes the important distinction between "incidence" and "prevalence": "Incidence refers to the number of new cases of a disease occurring in a population during a particular time interval; while prevalence refers to the total number of active cases of a disease present in a particular population during a particular time interval. Thus, prevalence includes new cases together with old cases who have either continuously remained ill or who have relapsed." Our discussion is based upon data referring to incidence, not prevalence.

types of deviant behavior, however, whites have a greater incidence rate than blacks. So far as we know, the racial differences in the incidence of pathological behavior that do exist are not caused by biological factors linked to race; instead, they are produced by the different life experiences of the two races.

1. Crime

Although all crime rates must be regarded as only estimates of actual incidence, it is clear that certain types of crime are much more common among blacks than among whites in the United States. Criminal homicide is a good example of this race differential: the black murder rate is estimated to be ten times as high as the white rate (see Pettigrew, 1964). Moreover, most of this killing is *intra*racial, not *inter*racial. Other types of crime, such as fraud and embezzlement, do *not* show significant racial differences. Furthermore, much of the "white-collar" crime among blacks is of a petty nature; whites generally occupy most of the white-collar positions where crimes such as large-scale embezzlement become a real possibility.

One reason why the true incidence of criminal behavior among blacks as compared to whites is impossible to determine is that most of our law enforcement machinery is controlled by whites, and in many locales arrests and sentences continue to be affected by the race of the individual committing the act. Assaults against blacks by blacks, for example, generally are dealt with more leniently than similar acts committed by blacks against whites. Blacks are well aware of this bias in the administration of justice, and this awareness surely must lower their respect for what many of them call "the white man's law."

In discussing crime, therefore, it is important to recognize that blacks do not always regard some of their acts as criminal even though they are so labeled by whites. (This, of course, touches upon the question of black versus white norms; see p. 69.) Stealing from white folks, for example, may be viewed as justifiable counteraggression against a foe who exploits blacks. This is particularly true when blacks learn that their chances for achieving redress in court for white exploitation may be almost nonexistent.

We must also recognize that in the ghettos crime may take on many of the trappings of a trade, the only trade that is readily open to an unskilled black who has received an inadequate education. In this context there is not the moral condemnation of criminal acts that one encounters in middle-class white society. There develops, then, the "hustler" who survives by victimizing others and who is not ostracized because he does not have an "honest" job. Indeed, as Malcolm X (1965) makes clear in his autobiography, becoming an effective hustler is probably the quickest way for the black youth to gain status and recognition in the ghetto. In psychological terms, living by one's wits receives a great deal of social reinforcement in such settings.

2. Psychoses

Severe aberrations in behavior that are called psychoses apparently occur more frequently among blacks than among whites, but no one can define the comparative incidence rates precisely. Some of the most carefully gathered and analyzed data pertaining to the relationship between race and psychotic behavior have been reported by Benjamin Malzberg (1944, pp. 373–395; 1953; 1959) based upon first admissions to hospitals in New York State. These data—as well as most data reported by others—do not include many individuals under private care (most of whom probably are white), nor those individuals, black and white alike, who are psychotic but are not under treatment.[32]

Nevertheless, it is clear that the incidence rates for certain types of psychoses are disproportionately high among blacks. Two of these are organic disorders, *paresis* (a consequence of syphilis) and *alcoholic psychosis*. Schizophrenia is also more common among blacks (Malzberg estimates a 2-to-1 black–white ratio) as is manic-depressive psychosis (for this syndrome, Malzberg estimates a 1.5-to-1 black–white ratio). In interpreting these data, Malzberg emphasizes that blacks are not biologically more vulnerable, rather he sees the environment as being responsible for their unfavorable mental health record. Special emphasis is placed on the fact that the majority of blacks in northern ghettos have migrated there from the rural South and are poorly prepared to cope with city life. The result, all too often, is a severe breakdown in behavior patterns, frequently helped along by drug addiction or the heavy use of alcohol.

3. Neuroses

Pettigrew (1964, p. 77) points out, correctly, that "If group data on psychosis are difficult to decipher, group data on neurosis are even more

[32] Indeed, admission rates to state hospitals provide a poor basis for arriving at any firm conclusions about the distribution of any type of aberrant behavior.

confusing." Nevertheless, later on (p. 77), he tentatively concludes that " . . . the ratio of Negro to white neuroticism is not as great as for the psychoses . . . ." Also, he predicts (p. 82) that in the future " . . . among Negro Americans, psychosis rates will begin to recede as neurosis rates climb steadily."

The central problem here, of course, is that behavioral scientists have not been able to establish criteria by means of which neurosis can be defined and identified satisfactorily in epidemiological studies. In the absence of such criteria, there is not much point in trying to determine how incidence rates compare for the two races. Even if we focus upon a particular symptom that neurotics frequently manifest, the available data frequently leave us confused. Take depression, for example. Two white psychiatrists, Arthur J. Prange, Jr. and M. M. Vitols (1962), report that depression is relatively uncommon in southern Negroes. They believe this to be true because depression is triggered by a sense of loss, and (p. 107) " . . . the southern Negro has less to lose and is less apt to lose it." In addition (p. 107), they suggest that Negroes have " . . . some culturally determined mechanisms for the management of losses which further reduce the likelihood of depression."

Considering the Prange–Vitols report, it comes as something of a surprise, then, to discover that depression is frequently mentioned as a symptom in the case studies cited by Grier and Cobbs in *Black Rage* (1969). Moreover, in discussing the psychology of black women, Grier and Cobbs emphasize their proneness to depressive reactions (p. 139). Can they be talking about the same people as Prange and Vitols?

We cannot be certain how to resolve what appears to be a clear discrepancy in these two reports. However, Prange and Vitols are specific in saying that their focus is on the *southern* Negro. While Grier and Cobbs do not define a geographical locale for their subjects, it is apparent that many of them were living in urban areas outside of the South when they were studied by these two black psychiatrists. However, many of their patients came out of the South and it is quite possible that the loss of their familiar supports served to precipitate their depressive reactions. Therefore, there may be no discrepancy between these two reports once the factor of situational context is taken into account. If this is true, Grier and Cobbs should modify their statements about depression in black females so that the significance of the geographical factor is acknowledged. We offer this only as an hypothesis, of course, for there may be other explanations of the apparent divergence between the two studies. It does illustrate, however, the kind of difficulty one encounters if he attempts to make interracial comparisons of neurotic behavior.

The Significance of the White Man's Perspective

Even a casual review of the literature on psychopathology as it is related to race suggests the difficulty of drawing valid conclusions at anything more than a very general level, and this is reflected in our discussion presented above. A basic reason for this state of affairs rests in the fact that almost all the judgments about psychopathology among black people have been rendered by white diagnosticians, and all too often the white professional has not been adequately trained to understand someone living in a subculture very different from his own. If we are concerned with paranoid behavior, for example, can we apply the same criteria to the black man as we do to the white man when the former is likely to experience more persecution and exploitation than the latter? But to make adjustments for cultural differences the diagnostician must have an intimate knowledge of what is "real" within a subculture and how that reality differs from what is true for the larger society. Unfortunately, most of us who are white lack this intimate knowledge of black culture. Therefore, our conclusions about particular forms of psychopathology among blacks are susceptible to considerable error.

1. The Black Norm (Grier and Cobbs)

In their discussion of mental illness, Grier and Cobbs assert that black Americans do develop—more extensively than whites—certain character traits which, in whites, are judged to be psychopathological. They also argue, however, that in blacks these traits are "adaptive devices" and must be judged against what they called the Black Norm. The meaning of this concept will become clearer if we quote at length from the authors themselves (1969, pp. 149–150):

We submit that it is necessary for a black man in America to develop a profound distrust of his white fellow citizens and of the nation. He must be on guard to protect himself against physical hurt. He must cushion himself against cheating, slander, humiliation, and outright mistreatment by the official representatives of society. If he does not so protect himself, he will live a life of such pain and shock as to find life itself unbearable. For his own survival, then, he must develop a *cultural paranoia* in which every white man is a potential enemy unless proved otherwise and every social system is set against him unless he personally finds out differently.

Every black man in America has suffered such injury as to be realistically sad about the hurt done him. He must, however, live in spite of the hurt and so he learns to know his tormentor exceedingly well. He develops a sadness and intimacy with misery which has become a characteristic of black Americans. It is a *cultural depression* and a *cultural masochism*.

He can never quite respect laws which have no respect for him, and laws designed to protect white men are viewed as white men's laws. To break another man's law may be inconvenient if one is caught and punished, but it can never have the moral consequences involved in breaking one's own law. The result may be described as a *cultural antisocialism*, but it is simply an accurate reading of one's environment—a gift black people have developed to a high degree, to keep alive.

These and related traits are simply adaptive devices developed in response to a peculiar environment. They are no more pathological than the compulsive manner in which a diver checks his equipment before a dive or a pilot his parachute. They represent normal devices for "making it" in America and clinicians who are interested in the psychological functioning of black people must get acquainted with this body of character traits which we call the *Black Norm*. It is a normal complement of psychological devices, and to find the amount of sickness a black man has, one must first total all that appears to represent illness and then subtract the Black Norm. What remains is illness and a proper subject for therapeutic endeavor. To regard the Black Norm as pathological and attempt to remove such traits by treatment would be akin to analyzing away a hunter's cunning or a banker's prudence. This is a body of characteristics essential to life for black men in America and woe be unto that therapist who does not recognize it.

In essence, then, Grier and Cobbs argue that blacks must develop certain traits which are commonly considered pathological if they are to adapt and survive in a hostile environment. In judging whether an individual black manifests psychopathology, then, we must refer to what is common or typical for blacks living in a hostile environment controlled by whites rather than to what is customary for whites.

CRIME!

2. A Black–White Comparison Using the MMPI

The importance of the concept of a *Black Norm* may also be illustrated by citing data gathered by administering the Minnesota Multiphasic Personality Inventory (MMPI). This test was originally devised to assist clinicians in making judgments about psychopathology, and it is generally regarded as the best test of its type. The use of the MMPI helps to overcome some of the subjectivity and bias of the individual clinician; however, we cannot rule out the possibility—as yet undemonstrated—of racial bias in the items that compose this test.[33]

In the Millfield study of southern rural children, the MMPI was administered to 258 eighth-grade children (52 white boys, 66 white girls, 59 black boys, and 81 black girls). Although most of the test items do not require more than a fifth-grade reading level to understand them, a tape-recorded form of the MMPI was prepared for use in this study. This enabled the children to hear each item being read aloud while they were simultaneously reading it in the test booklet.

The scoring of the MMPI is both objective and reliable. While many different scores can be generated from the answers of subjects to MMPI test items, our interest here is in how black and white children compared in the scores they received on the 10 clinical scales that are most often used in the interpretation of MMPI data. These scales are numbered one through zero in Figures 17 and 18 where the mean scores of white boys are compared to those of black boys and those of white girls with those of black girls, respectively.

The scoring of the MMPI was standardized—separately for the two sexes—by using groups of normal men and women (no blacks were included in these normative samples). Arbitrarily, the mean score for both males and females was made equivalent to 50 on each of the 10 clinical

[33] For a brief description of the construction and history of the MMPI, see Chapter 11 in Baughman and Dahlstrom (1968).

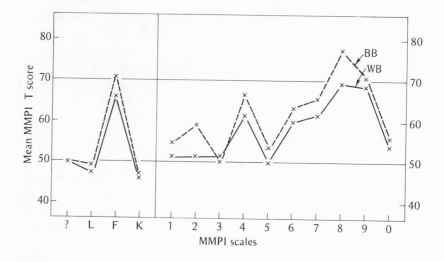

Fig. 17. Mean MMPI profiles of eighth-grade white boys (WB) and eighth-grade black boys (BB). (From Baughman & Dahlstrom, 1968.)

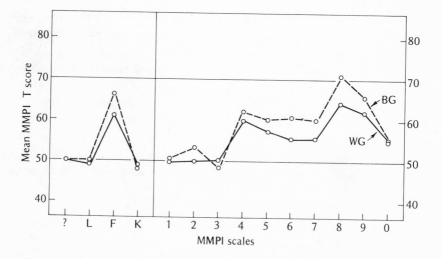

Fig. 18. Mean MMPI profiles of eighth-grade white girls (WG) and eighth-grade black girls (BG). (From Baughman & Dahlstrom, 1968.)

scales. Therefore, the degree of the departure of any individual (or the mean of any group) from the average of the Minnesota normal group on any of the scales can be gauged by how far their scores depart from 50 in Figures 17 and 18.

Figure 17 shows that on 9 of the 10 clinical scales the mean score of the black boys departs more from normal than is true for the mean score of the white boys. Only on Scale 3—which attempts to measure hysterical tendencies—is there a slight reversal of this overall pattern. And, as Figure 18 shows, the results are highly similar when white girls are compared with black girls.

If these results are taken at face value, we would have to conclude that, on the average, there is more psychopathology among the black adolescents than among their white counterparts.[34] If we accept the Grier—Cobbs argument, however, we would have to conclude that the black scores are inflated because they include a cultural component in addition to the personal. But, if so, *how much* of the discrepancy between black and white scores can be assigned to cultural variation? At present, this question—referring to *degree* or *quantity*—cannot be answered.

Many experts in the measurement of personality recoil from the idea that we might have to have separate test norms for blacks and whites on an instrument like the MMPI. Yet it is true that the MMPI was developed using separate norms for the two sexes because, *empirically*, this was found to be necessary. Therefore, we also need to keep an open mind with regard to the possible need for separate norms for blacks and whites. The key question, of course, is whether or not a given score on a particular scale has the same or different behavioral implications for blacks and whites. Only careful empirical studies can provide us with a sound answer to this perplexing problem.[35]

[34]Other black-white comparisons based upon the MMPI have given similar results; for example, see Hokanson and Calden (1960) and McDonald and Gynther (1962).

[35]Although Figures 17 and 18 are presented only in the interest of the general point that we have just made, the Scale 2 findings do reflect upon an earlier part of our discussion. Scale 2 aims at detecting depressive trends in the personality; the results suggest that such trends may be more pronounced among black adolescents than among white. But whereas Grier and Cobbs (1969) emphasize the depressive component in the black female, these MMPI data indicate that such trends are stronger among black males.

Treatment

Broadly speaking, psychopathological behavior is treated either by *physical* or *verbal* techniques—or by a combination of the two. In the former, we include such procedures as electroshock and the prescription of therapeutic drugs; the latter ranges from classical psychoanalysis to confrontation groups (all of which we shall include under the rubric of *psychotherapy*).

There is a significant relationship between social class and the type of treatment emotionally disturbed individuals receive (see Hollingshead & Redlich, 1958; also, Myers & Roberts, 1959). Thus, a person from the middle or upper class is more likely to receive some type of psychotherapy—either as the sole treatment administered or in combination with some form of physical therapy—than is an individual from the lower class. Lower-class patients more frequently are restricted to some type of physical therapy; when they cannot be treated on an outpatient basis, they usually are confined to large public hospitals where the physical therapy is supplemented with little more than custodial care.

Because of the situation just sketched, it should come as no surprise to the reader to learn that blacks, comparatively speaking, seldom are the recipients of psychotherapeutic efforts. This is one area, however, where blacks may not recognize that they are discriminated against in the delivery of essential health services. For, like lower-class persons of all colors, they tend to understand a pill, a shot, or some other type of tangible therapeutic intervention much better than they comprehend the relevance of an offer to "talk over what's bothering you." Indeed, disturbed blacks may feel that they *are* being discriminated against if a professional worker offers "talk" instead of a pill, especially if the professional worker is white.

Obviously, this does not mean that we have *no* experience with blacks in psychotherapeutic situations. The classical psychotherapeutic techniques (psychoanalysis, for example), however, were developed primarily while working with disturbed whites. Moreover, these whites generally were well educated and had good verbal resources. With blacks who have comparable backgrounds and talents, the same psychotherapeutic techniques may be applied with equal hopes of success (there is one important qualification to this statement; see p. 75). However, vast numbers of blacks in need of treatment for emotional disturbances do not have backgrounds that prepare them well for treatment efforts which are primarily verbal in nature.

Even with blacks who might profit from some type of psychotherapy, there is a difficulty they face in achieving this end that is not encountered by whites, as we anticipated above. We refer here to the fact that the vast majority of professionals trained to offer such services are white; there are, for example, relatively few black psychologists and psychiatrists. The white professional (who is usually of middle-class origins) commonly has only a limited awareness of the black experience, and most blacks readily sense this limitation. Moreover, the black's entire history is such that he finds it extremely difficult (perhaps impossible) to trust whites, including those who offer psychotherapeutic services (see St. Clair, 1951). We have here, then, a situation that is stacked against psychotherapeutic success: a nontrusting patient interacting with a therapist whose awareness of his patient's world is limited, or even distorted.

When a black does commit himself to the psychotherapeutic task, there are additional problems tied to his racial identity that must be overcome if he is to benefit from the experience. Walter Adams (1950), a black psychiatrist, emphasized two of these in his discussion of the black patient in psychiatric treatment. First of all, according to Adams (p. 309), ". . . a Negro patient uses race as an unconscious defense to conceal more basic conflicts." Second (p. 310), the therapist may ". . . oversimplify and . . . ascribe all problems of Negro patients to cultural and racial conflict." Black therapists, as well as white therapists, may make this "racial error" in coping with black patients, particularly if the therapists themselves have a high degree of race consciousness.

Even this sketchy treatment of psychotherapy should make clear the nature of the difficulties that must be overcome if such services are to be made available to black people, and there is little basis for optimism. The highest priority, we believe, should be given to the recruitment and training of blacks to deliver such services; no matter how well intentioned the white professional may be, he is likely to encounter suspicion and hostility in his work with blacks that will subvert his effectiveness.

Chapter 7/Socialization and the Family

Although we must not neglect the genetic determinants of behavior, it is clear that most behavior which has either interpersonal or intrapersonal significance derives to a significant degree from the socialization experiences of the individual. For most persons the formative socialization experiences occur within the family context; consequently, the family is viewed as a prime determinant of individual behavior. The history of the black American family differs markedly from that of the white American family, and even today there are important differences between the typical black and the typical white family. In this section we shall summarize black—white similarities and differences in family structure—as well as their socialization techniques—in order to give added perspective to the topics that were discussed earlier.

Origins of Black Families: A Post-Slavery Phenomenon

In 1965 the United States Department of Labor published a report on black families that immediately received widespread attention and became the focal point of considerable controversy. This monograph, prepared under the direction of Daniel P. Moynihan, is commonly called the Moynihan study or report. Its central theme is suggested by the following quotations taken from it:

At the heart of the deterioration of the fabric of Negro society is the deterioration of the Negro family. It is the fundamental source of the weakness of the Negro community at the present time (p. 5).

The white family has achieved a high degree of stability and is maintaining that stability. By contrast, the family structure of lower class Negroes is highly unstable, and in many urban centers is approaching complete breakdown (p. 5).

There is no one Negro problem. There is no one solution. Nonetheless, at the center of the tangle of pathology is the weakness of the family structure (p. 30).

Moynihan provides the reader with a great amount of statistical data organized to support his conclusion about the troubled state of black families; some of these data will be cited in the following section.

If we accept monogamy (only one marriage at a time during life) as the desired social condition, and if it is beneficial to children to be reared by their natural parents who remain together for life, it is clear from the data summarized by Moynihan that more black than white children grow up in undesirable family situations. Unfortunately, however, Moynihan's presentation so accentuates the negative in black family life that it must put blacks on the defensive—and it is difficult to respond constructively if one is on the defensive. In point of fact, given the history of black Americans, one could just as well emphasize their tremendous achievement with respect to family structure. We say this because family life as white America knows it was unknown to the great majority of blacks during slavery (see Frazier, 1939). In less than 100 years, however, they have achieved a measure of family organization and stability that is truly remarkable considering the disadvantaged circumstances under which they were forced to live even after they became "free" (see Bernard, 1966). To emphasize the fact that proportionately more black families than white families are "disorganized"—as Moynihan does—fails to give proper emphasis to a real black achievement in this regard. To be fair, however, we must acknowledge that Moynihan is not alone in his emphasis. For example, E. Franklin Frazier, the eminent black authority on the black family, made similar comments much earlier (1950, p. 276):

As the result of family disorganization a large proportion of Negro children and youth have not undergone the socialization which only the family can provide. The disorganized families have failed to provide for their emotional needs and have not provided the discipline and habits which are necessary for personality development. Because the disorganized family has failed in its function as a socializing agency, it has handicapped the children in their relations to the institutions in the community.

In analyses like those of Moynihan and Frazier the emphasis is upon the disorganized family as the source or *cause* of various types of problem behavior. We must also recognize, however, that there is no direct or simple way to create greater numbers of stable families since the type of family which does emerge depends upon a very complex network of social conditions. Thus, while the family may produce behavior forms, it is also the product of larger social forces that are extremely difficult to change.

Family Structure

There are several characteristics of black family structure that have been emphasized by students of this topic. In this section we shall define the most salient of these.

1. Rural—Urban Differences

To begin, it is important to recognize that black family life has been especially vulnerable to urbanization. Although significant numbers of blacks continue to live in the rural South, vast numbers have migrated to urban centers in the North, South, and West. Indeed, blacks are more urbanized than whites (U.S. Department of Labor, 1965); only 20% of black Americans now live in the rural South.

However, the "family roots" of most black Americans can be traced to the rural South. And the life that blacks lived there—the education they received, the skills they learned—prepared them poorly for the complexities of city living. It should come as no surprise, therefore, that many families disintegrated when they moved to the city. Furthermore, many individual males who might have established and maintained families in a rural setting were unable to do so in urban centers. As a consequence, disorganization among black families is much more prevalent in urban than in rural areas (Baughman & Dahlstrom, 1968; Bernard, 1966; U.S. Department of Labor, 1965).

2. Size

A basic fact of life for the black child is that he is likely to be socialized in a much larger family than is the white child. Census data show, for example, that the fertility rate for black women is about 40% higher than it is for white women. Furthermore, among black families there is an inverse correlation between family income and the number of children: the less the income, the greater the number of children (U.S. Department of Labor, 1965). An obvious consequence of this situation is that the monetary resources available for the training and education of the typical black child are pitifully small.

Between one-fifth and one-fourth of the black children are born out of wedlock, whereas 50 years ago this figure was closer to one-tenth (Bernard, 1966). There are those who attribute this increase in illegitimacy to the desire of black women to collect funds from the Aid for Dependent Children (AFDC) program; however, there is no evidence that such motivation exists (except in the exceptional case) nor that such motivation is more common among black than among white women. As Bernard points out (1966, p. 39), ". . . modern Negro women . . . do not value large families."

The Baughman—Dahlstrom study (1968, p. 357) in the rural South provides data which are in agreement with Bernard's conclusion. When 64 black mothers of kindergarten-age children were asked if they had been pleased to discover they were pregnant with the child, 59% said no. Of 77 white mothers who were asked the same question, only 23% gave a negative answer. The clear implication in this study was that many more black than white children had begun life unwanted by their mothers, a condition that very likely had far reaching effects upon their life experiences.

3. Extended Families

The evidence also shows that black children are more likely to grow up in extended families than are white children. That is, their households are more likely to contain individuals who are not either their parents or their siblings. Frequently these individuals are relatives, but often the black household contains individuals who are not related to the family. For example, they may be roomers or boarders who are there because of the economic requirements of the family. For the growing child there are two primary consequences of this situation. First, the composition of the household is a changing thing so that he is not certain who will be present tomorrow. Second, his socialization is affected by individuals who may share in the child-rearing tasks but who do not have the same commitment to him that we ordinarily find in parents who head a nonextended family.

4. Fatherless Families

A significant factor in the lives of large numbers of black children is that they grow up in families headed by women. Census data show, for example, that at any given time approximately one-fourth of the black families are without a male head. This is a rate that is almost three times that found in the white community (U.S. Department of Labor, 1965). Furthermore, we must recognize that children who are living in a family with a male head when the census is taken may at other times live in a setting where there is no man present. Finally, the probability that a black child will be living in a family headed by a woman is much greater in urban than in rural settings (Baughman & Dahlstrom, 1968).

The relatively high incidence of father-absence must be regarded as a negative factor as far as the socialization of black children is concerned. Nevertheless, in individual cases this general conclusion may not hold. If the husband is unemployed, for example, and is an additional economic burden for his wife, the situation within the family may improve for the child if the father leaves. And employment is an acute problem for the black male, especially in urban centers.

5. The Concept of Matriarchy

As H. H. Hyman and J. S. Reed observed in a recent paper on black matriarchy (1969, p. 346), "The American Negro family has been characterized as a *matriarchy* so often that the assertion is widely accepted as a truth rather than a proposition still in need of empirical evidence and critical analysis." Our own research, as well as that of one of our students (see Bridgette below), leads us to agree with Hyman and Reed that a reconsideration of the concept of black matriarchy is overdue.

What is a matriarchal family? The simplest definition—and one that is frequently used—is that it is a family headed by a female. Such families are more prevalent in the black than in the white community, as we have just seen. This does not mean, however, that the *typical* black family can be described as one having a female head. Indeed, at any given time about three-fourths of the black families are headed by males. By this simple criterion, then, it is correct to conclude that matriarchy is more common in the black than in the white community, but not that matriarchy is typical of black families.

Intact families may also be described as matriarchal ". . . if the wife exercises predominant influence over family affairs (Hyman & Reed, 1969, p. 346)." Valid data pertaining to husband—wife dominance is very difficult to generate, but Hyman and Reed present findings from three survey studies which indicate that the influence of black wives in the decision-making process is no greater than that of white wives. They question, therefore, the assertion that intact black families are more matriarchal than intact white families.

In the Millfield study parental dominance was evaluated in interviews with 136 eighth-grade children (28 white boys, 30 white girls, 32 black boys, 46 black girls). When asked who makes the decision when the parents disagree over what the subject should do, more blacks than whites said father (53% versus 29%, respectively). In response to the more general question of who was boss in the family, the blacks again chose father more often than the whites (84% versus 76%, respectively). Clearly, these data, like those analyzed by Hyman and Reed, run contrary to the designation of intact black families as matriarchal.

Even more recently, Bridgette (1970), as part of his study of self-esteem, asked 254 rural and village children in North Carolina to answer 13 questions about their parents. These children were in the eleventh grade of a desegregated school; there were 80 white boys, 82 white girls, 39 black boys, and 53 black girls. The questions were of the following type: Comparing your mother and father, who usually makes the rules for you? Who is the boss at home? Who seems proud of the things you do? Who usually punishes you? For each of the 13 questions, the subject had to choose one of four answers: mother, father, neither, or both.

Children of *both* races selected mother as their answer to these questions much more often than father. In doing so, they indicated more day-to-day involvement with their mothers than with their fathers. Although this pattern characterized the responses of both races, it was more pronounced among the black children. There were also significant

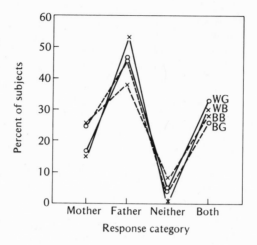

Fig. 19. Percent of eleventh-grade children in each of four race—sex groups choosing each of four answers to the question "Comparing your mother and father, who is the boss at home?" WB = white boys. WG = white girls. BB = black boys. BG = black girls. (From Bridgette, 1970.)

sex differences within both races and indications that the white boys were more closely involved with their fathers than the black boys were with their fathers. In short, the day-to-day worlds of these children were mother-centered, and this was more true for the black children than for the white children.

It is especially interesting, then, to note how these children responded to the question, "Comparing your mother and father, who is the boss at home?" To this question, as Figure 19 shows, proportionately more children of *both* races answered father rather than mother. This would seem to indicate that they attribute ultimate authority to father even though it is mother who is more controlling of and involved with their day-to-day behavior. We must also note a small race difference: white children more often than black children reported that father was boss. This trend runs counter to that reported by Baughman and Dahlstrom; however, statistically, this race difference is not significant (see Bridgette, 1970).

In our judgment, the data that we have presented in this section force us to question the validity of the proposition that intact black families are *markedly* more matriarchal than intact white families. At the very least, the proposition needs to be carefully reexamined using a variety of data gathered in both rural and urban settings and at various socioeconomic levels. As Grier and Cobbs observe (1969, p. 51), "The simplistic view of the black family as a matriarchy is an unfortunate theme repeated too often by scholars who should know better."

6. Two Types of Families: Respectable and Nonrespectable

A number of observers of black America have emphasized the deep cleavage that exists between blacks committed to a so-called respectable way of life and those who apparently are content to follow the "low road" (see Frazier, 1939, 1962; Drake & Cayton, 1962; Clark, 1965). Jessie Bernard, in her study of marriage and family among blacks, puts it this way (1966, p. 27):

> However little agreement there may be among students of Negro society in other respects, there is remarkable unanimity about the existence of two distinct strands in that society: one is generally called the "respectable" strand; the other is variously referred to as the "masses," the "low life," the "nonrespectable" strand. This distinction is especially significant for any understanding of family patterns among Negroes, because the important characteristics of each strand concern morals, propriety, and family life.[36]

It must be emphasized that the respectable–nonrespectable distinction is not simply another way of identifying social-class levels; as Bernard points out, both strands are to be found at every class level within the black community.

The words "respectable" and "nonrespectable" have value connotations, of course, and this is one reason why some students of black culture select other terms to refer to the distinction that is being made (Bernard proposes "acculturated" and "externally adapted"). In our judgment, however, none of the alternatives appear to be very satisfactory nor do we see any particular advantage to be gained by removing value connotations. As usually used, "respectable" refers to individuals or groups (such as a family) committed to the control of impulse expression (particularly with respect to sexual and drinking behavior), to a stable family life, to honest

[36] Jessie Bernard, *Marriage and Family among Negroes.* © 1966, Prentice Hall, Inc.

work, and so on. "Nonrespectables," in contrast, tend to the immediate discharge of impulse, or to what Frazier (1949, p. 190) calls "free and uncontrolled behavior." Whereas the respectables are likely to be described as puritanical, the nonrespectables are likely to be called hedonistic or pleasure-seeking.

We are discussing a typology, of course, and typologies always create difficulties for behavioral scientists. This is because in practice many individuals or groups do not fit neatly into any of the categories (in this instance, two). Furthermore, in the present instance, to the extent that the typology has usefulness, there is no obvious reason why it may not be applied to whites as well as blacks. If this were done, the literature on the black would suggest that the respectable/nonrespectable ratio would be higher among whites than among blacks. That is, the prevalence rate for nonrespectables would be higher in the black community than in the white.

The distinction that is being made here has special meaning for respectables (or would-be respectables) who find themselves trapped in urban ghettos. Childrearing under these circumstances becomes extremely difficult as parents attempt to prevent their children from drifting into the nonrespectable way of life which seems to inundate them. A very graphic picture of the "low road" is presented by Malcolm X in his autobiography (1965), as is a description of what is necessary if one is to renounce this way of life. To be effective such renunciation must develop within the black community under black leadership. Although many whites (and blacks) find it easy to criticize the Black Muslims, they must be given credit for demonstrating that such renunciation is possible. At the heart of their program is a commitment to a stable family life and the rejection of immediate impulse gratification.

Socialization Techniques

In all cultures and with all races a variety of techniques are used to socialize children. Sometimes these techniques are used deliberately; on other occasions the user is not aware of what he is doing as far as his influence on a child is concerned. In this section we shall examine several socialization techniques as they apply to the black American.

1. Imitation and Modeling

A child develops a significant portion of his behavioral repertoire by imitating persons in his environment (see Bandura and Walters, 1963). Generally speaking, parents are aware of children's imitative tendencies and this is one reason why some parents are deeply concerned with the company their children keep. Especially in the ghetto, parents who value "respectability" are faced with an extremely difficult problem, for their children are surrounded by individuals who are inappropriate models. Also, there is a special problem in fatherless families; both boys and girls have a more difficult time learning appropriate sex-role behavior when there is no adult male in the family.

In day-to-day living much imitation takes place without anyone attending to it. But many parents do deliberately concern themselves with this process; thus, they urge a child to be like "Uncle John" but not to be like "Aunt Clara." It is very difficult to judge how effective such instruction is, but we can determine empirically what emphasis parents believe they place upon the imitative process. In the Millfield study, for example, mothers of kindergarten-age children were asked a series of questions to determine if they pointed to themselves, the child's siblings, his grandparents, other relatives, or his playmates as models to copy. Also, they were asked if they ever used someone as a negative model ("Don't be like him").

Many more black than white mothers said they used the child's parents as models (74% versus 46%, respectively). The same trend appeared for the use of siblings as models, although mothers said they used siblings in this way much less frequently than they used parents (34% of the black mothers reported using siblings as models versus 17% of the white mothers). Also, more black than white mothers acknowledged using negative models (53% versus 28%, respectively). As far as the use of grandparents, other relatives, and playmates was concerned, there were no significant racial differences. The trends in these data, however, were in the same direction as the differences just reported.

If these racial differences in the mothers' reports correspond to actual behavioral differences in the homes—and we cannot be certain that they do—what do they suggest? One possibility, it seems to us, is that the black mothers, more than the white mothers, believe that there are undesirable models in the child's immediate environment; by their verbal instructions they may be trying to point the child away from the "bad" and toward the "good."[37]

2. Reward and Punishment (Reinforcement)

Parents commonly attempt to influence the behavior of their children by administering rewards and punishments. Some parents are "thin" on rewards and "heavy" on punishments, whereas other parents manifest a reverse ratio. Generally speaking, developmental psychologists agree that a training regime which emphasizes the positive reinforcement (that is, rewarding) of desirable behavior leads to the most desirable long-term outcomes.

There are social-class differences in the relative emphasis placed upon the use of rewards and punishments in child-training (see Kamii, 1965, Hess, Shipman, & Jackson, 1965). Punishment, for example, usually occupies a more prominent position in the child-training practices of lower-class families than in middle- and upper-class families. The latter, in contrast, feature rewards—both verbal (praise) and material—more than the former. It is not surprising, then, that proportionately more black than white mothers in the Millfield study expressed the opinion that whipping was good for a child (94% versus 78%, respectively). In contrast, 86% of the white mothers but only 70% of the black mothers said they believed in praising children.

Training to Be a Black. Grier and Cobbs, in their clinical analysis, emphasize that black mothers frequently are punitive and cruel, especially in their relationships with their sons. Black mothers are this way, Grier and Cobbs argue, because they see it as a means of creating an adult who can survive in a hostile, white-controlled world. This maternal pattern had its origins in the conditions of slavery (Grier & Cobbs, 1969, pp. 143–144):

It is reported that newly captured African women slew their children rather than have them reared as slaves. Their decision was a

---

[37]Consistent with this interpretation is the fact that when eighth-grade children living in the same general locale were interviewed, only black children reported that there was too much drinking and too many "bad" nightspots in their area. (The latter were patronized only by blacks since a segregated way of life was enforced in the area.)

significant one for us, because the infanticide speaks clearly of her knowledge of the options—*she* must kill her child, for if she lets him live it is *she* who must raise him to be a slave. Once the mother opts for her child's life she assumes the task of conveying to him the nature of the world in which he will live and teaching him how to survive in it. In effect, she had to take the role of slave master, treat the child with *capricious cruelty, hurt him physically and emotionally* [italics ours], and demand that he respond in an obsequious helpless manner—a manner she knew would enhance his chances of survival. She had to take particular pains to crush any defiant, aggressive traits.

It was aggression, then, that had to be eradicated, for aggression would lead to counteraggression and even destruction by the white man.

The present world of the black American is not quite as threatening as it used to be; however, one can hardly describe it as benign. Moreover, once child-training practices are adopted by members of a group, they change only slowly.[38] It is consistent, then, to find that the black mothers in the Millfield study said that they whipped their children for aggressive behavior more than for any other reason. Furthermore, proportionately more black than white mothers reported whipping their children for being aggressive (61% versus 37%, respectively).[39] Inconsistent with the Grier–Cobbs thesis, however, was a tendency for more mothers of black girls to report whipping them for aggression than was true for the mothers of black boys (65% versus 56%, respectively).

Although social conditions are changing, undoubtedly large numbers of black parents will continue to train their children to be blacks. Many black leaders see this as a desirable objective; of course, they are also very much aware of the critical importance of *redefining* what it means to be a black, and this means rewarding rather than punishing behavior which evidences pride in blackness.

[38] Of significance in this regard is Bernard's observation (1966, p. 107) "... that relatively fewer Negro than white mothers, class for class, have been exposed to child-rearing experts."

[39] Whipping for aggression within the home may actually increase the child's aggressive behavior, since the parent, in whipping, provides a model that the child may later imitate.

3. Inculcation of Goals and Aspirations

One of the most critical aspects of socialization involves the development of goals or aspirations, especially with respect to education and
work. Most white middle-class children are surrounded by individuals
whose life styles influence them to set high goals in this regard, although,
clearly, these life styles are being subjected to serious challenge at the
present time. Black children, in contrast, have *relatively few* models
available to them as far as high educational and vocational achievements
are concerned. The typical adult in the black world has an education that
is inferior to that of the white and a job that is less prestigious and
provides less monetary return.

All American children, however, are bombarded with messages stress-
ing the importance of getting a "good education." And, at least at the
verbal level, this message reaches blacks as effectively as it does whites.
Indeed, a recent review of research in this domain (U.S. Department of
Health, Education, and Welfare, 1968, p. 25) concludes that "Vocational
and educational aspirations have generally been found to be . . . higher for
Negroes than whites within class levels." Consistent with this conclusion is
the Baughman–Dahlstrom finding based upon interviews with eighth-grade
children. Sixty percent of the black children compared to 34% of the
white children said they wanted to go to college. Moreover, significantly
more black than white children expressed the belief that a college
education was necessary for the kind of work they wanted to do (84%
versus 61%, respectively).

Unfortunately, a large percentage of the children who express high
educational and vocational aspirations do not have a realistic understanding of what kind of educational program they must follow if their
vocational goal is to be achieved. Also, frequently their stated educational
aims are not consistent either with their abilities or their previous
educational attainments. Oftentimes black parents cannot provide realistic
guidance for their children in these areas because they are unfamiliar with
job and advanced educational requirements. In the Millfield study, for
example, 67% of the black mothers said they wanted their children to
enter a profession, but only 40% of them wanted their children to attend
college. Nor are teachers as helpful in this regard as one might expect them
to be. Thus, although 47 black eighth-grade children in the same study said
they wanted to go to college, only three reported that their teachers had

talked to them about college. Such data underscore the tremendous need that exists in the black community for competent guidance with respect to educational and vocational opportunities. There has been a sharp increase in such opportunities for blacks, but blacks are not yet receiving adequate information and guidance so that they can take full advantage of these new opportunities.

Finally, we should note one meaningful way in which the job desires of black students differ from those of white students. As data gathered by Singer and Stefflre (1956) show, whites more often than blacks refer to the importance of securing "a very interesting job." Blacks, in contrast, are more likely than whites to emphasize the importance of obtaining a job "which you are absolutely sure of keeping." This finding is not surprising, of course, inasmuch as it is commonly recognized in the black community that blacks are the last to be hired but the first to be fired. This prejudice continues to exist in many job situations, yet it is also true that social conditions have changed enough so that there are a significant number of situations (both vocational and educational in nature) where the black can take advantage of a type of reverse discrimination. Young blacks need to be guided into these new opportunities so that they can both advance their own interests and secure bases from which they can offer leadership to the remainder of the black community.

Chapter 8/Final Comments:
Leadership and Education

One cannot examine blacks psychologically without concluding that the effects of oppression are to be found in almost all sectors of their lives. Surely this should not surprise us, for even today the black American does not experience freedom in the same sense that it is known to the white American. Indeed, considering the black American's history we may consider it remarkable that his psychological problems are not more numerous than they are.

Nevertheless, there is no denying the fact that the data we have reviewed indicate that in a number of behavioral domains the difficulties of blacks exceed those of whites.[40] Some comparative data are surprising, however, especially those data pertaining to self-esteem and the locus of

---

[40] We cannot emphasize too much that we are talking about "blacks in general" and not *particular* blacks. Whenever we refer to a link between race and behavior, it is absolutely essential to remember that we are referring only to group trends; because a particular person is black does not mean that he manifests the behavior referred to. Group trends are very important, however, since they must be taken into account in social planning and action-type programs as well as in the conduct of established programs, such as the public schools. Unfortunately, many such programs do not provide adequately for the variability that exists within the black community with respect to particular behaviors. Thus, for example, the bright black child may be smothered by a school system geared to a much lower average level of performance.

authority or power in intact families. If nothing else, such findings should prod us to constant reexamination of concepts that are applied to the racial scene. Although social structures and personal behavior are slow to change, change does take place. Only constant attention to behavioral data will ensure that our concepts involving race actually are in accord with current data.

Most people who study the linkage between race and behavior do so because of concern about how the unresolved problems in this domain continue to eat at the very foundation of our country. It should be clear to all of us by now that we are not going to discover any quick or easy solutions to these problems, no matter how hard we may wish for them. It is relevant at this point, however, to consider two basic needs that must be met if we dare hope for even long-term resolutions of racial conflict: these are the need for the development of black leadership and the need for an altered and improved approach to education.

Leadership

Within the black community there is a tremendous need for leadership at every level. And this leadership must be black; well-meaning whites will not do. The cynicism which is so pervasive in the black makeup after centuries of exploitation simply will not permit most blacks to respond to white leadership, even if on occasion it is sincere and not motivated by self-interest.

Unfortunately, however, once a psychological characteristic or process such as cynicism is established in a person it tends to generalize. Thus, blacks who mistrust white leadership because of its self-serving quality also tend to mistrust black leadership for the same reason. The black is likely, therefore, to become a true cynic in the sense that he comes to believe that human conduct, irrespective of race, is motivated completely by self-interest.

As long as blacks maintain such attitudes, efforts to solve problems in the black community are likely to be ineffective. To change these attitudes, blacks must witness first-hand their leaders working among them with the black community's interest as their central concern. This means, we believe, that black youths must be educated and trained so that they will seek leadership positions in the black community; education and training must not be looked upon merely as a way to escape from the black community into the white man's affluent society. Such education and training will make black youths aware of their people's history and develop in them an understanding of the psychological processes which are characteristic of blacks. Hopefully, out of such understanding can emerge the development of leadership techniques which will overcome the mistrust which is so pervasive among blacks.

Is there a role for whites in the development of black leadership? There is, indeed, a role for whites, and an important one. But it is also a circumscribed role, and whites must accept the need for restraint no matter how lofty they may consider their motives to be. Most of all, they must resist the temptation to be the puppeteer, to be the power that moves the black man who is out front posing as a leader. Rather, whites in positions of influence and power must ensure that the developing black leadership secures access to the resources which must be used if the problems of the black community are to be solved. Blacks can solve their basic problems under black leadership, but they must gain access to the broader resources of our society without being forced to act as the "white man's nigger." It is the responsibility of white leadership to see that the black leadership obtains this access.

Education

Of all the concerns of black leadership, none should have a higher priority than education. And education must be broadly conceived; not just as a formal process that begins when a child reaches age six.

Many critics of the Supreme Court's 1954 school desegregation decision were incensed when the Court cited research by social scientists in support of its opinion that schools could not be separate *and* equal. This was a sound position, however, and one that should have been taken much earlier. On the other hand, the Supreme Court's actions implementing this decision are open, we believe, to rather severe criticism. But this may be an unfair position to take; if criticism is to be levelled, perhaps it should be directed at social and behavioral scientists for not providing the Court with a more adequate body of knowledge to use in guiding its efforts at implementation of its desegregation decision. Consistent with history, blacks—especially black children—have suffered most as a consequence of the path that has been followed since 1954.

At the time this is being written, many school districts are under court orders to completely desegregate their systems at every grade level—*immediately*. This means, of course, that these districts—along with many others—continued their segregated practices for more than a full school generation after the 1954 decision. Given this record of noncompliance, it is just a little difficult to respond sympathetically to the cry that more time is needed to plan adequately for desegregation. To the extent that chaos does ensue, it seems to us that the basic responsibility for this state of affairs rests upon the local citizenry in the affected school districts.

Unfortunately, attributing blame or responsibility does nothing to help the children who must cope with the resulting situation. And very real educational problems are created for both white and black children by instant desegregation at every grade level. We do not know how to cope with many of these problems; moreover, many solutions that might be attempted are ruled out unless the educational system is given a massive increase in funds. There is no evidence that the schools will secure such additional resources in the foreseeable future, at least on the massive scale that is needed. Most school systems were insufficiently funded prior to desegregation; now their problems are multiplied without an appropriate increase in funding.

The problem of the black child is particularly acute in all of this, especially in the upper grades. Instantly desegregated at the advanced levels, only a relatively few blacks find that their academic preparation has been adequate to prepare them to compete on equal terms with whites of the same grade level. This discovery—and it does come as a genuine surprise to many blacks—can only be demoralizing and shattering of self-confidence. Threatened by the situation, many blacks must react defensively and angrily at "the system," creating turmoil in the process. Even if their white teachers and white classmates want to help—and many clearly do not—the black child's previous experiences dispose him to mistrust their motivations and set him to resist their offers of assistance. The polarization that results creates a situation in the schools that functions to the educational disadvantage of blacks and whites alike. The blacks achieve desegregation, but not the kind of educational experience they seek.

Some of these problems could have been avoided if the Supreme Court in 1954 had ordered immediate desegregation of all first grades as the initial step in a "grade-per-year" desegregation plan. Such a procedure would have achieved desegregation at a much faster rate than has been achieved by the path the Court followed, and it would have lessened the problems associated with instant desegregation at advanced grade levels. Furthermore, it could have been combined with a freedom-of-choice order for the advanced grades so that some black children who were prepared could have availed themselves of the opportunities provided by such an order.[41]

Events run their course and perhaps it is too late to institute the combination plan just described. Black leaders who proposed its adoption at this late date might continue to be black but not leaders. In our judgment, however, the evidence indicates that its adoption even now would be advantageous to black children. Perhaps the black leadership should offer to support such an alteration in the desegregation machinery *in exchange for an expansion of the educational program that would be directed at a critical educational need of the black community.* We refer here to the need for a *great* expansion in preschool training within the black community. The early socialization of so many black children simply does not prepare them for entry into the school system, whether that system is segregated or desegregated (see Deutsch *et al.,* 1968; also, Baughman & Dahlstrom, 1968). To the schools, these children pose a problem in rehabilitation from the time they enter the schools' doors; they cannot be properly educated by the standard techniques which are now used with them. Headstart is a beginning effort to meet this need, but blacks should call it what it is—tokenism. A massive rather than a token effort is needed; in our judgment, this is a more critical educational need of blacks than is immediate desegregation across the board at advanced grade levels.

---

[41] We are fully aware of the fact that some academically qualified black students would not have been able to take advantage of such an order because of the fear of reprisal from the white community, directed in some form at either themselves or their parents. In our judgment, however, this loss to the black community would have been much less than blacks have experienced by the course that has been followed. We must also recognize that the Supreme Court may have been reluctant to specify *how* desegregation was to be accomplished, a function that many competent authorities insist is a legislative responsibility. However, the Court could have indicated—at least in subsequent rulings—that the combination plan which we have described would be viewed as one acceptable way of carrying out its 1954 mandate.

Suggested Readings

Elizabeth W. Miller's, *The Negro in America: A Bibliography* (1966), is a useful guide to articles and books about black Americans. For a review of comparative psychological studies of blacks and whites, two articles by Ralph M. Dreger and Kent S. Miller (1960, 1968) should be consulted.

Several "broad-band" books provide a great deal of source material on black Americans: Gunnar Myrdal's, *An American Dilemma* (1944, 1962); E. Franklin Frazier's, *The Negro in the United States* (1949, 1957); Talcott Parsons' and Kenneth B. Clark's (Eds.), *The Negro American* (1966); and, Thomas F. Pettigrew's, *A Profile of the Negro American* (1964). For an emphasis on psychological development, *Social Class, Race, and Psychological Development* (1968; Martin Deutsch, Irwin Katz, and Arthur R. Jensen, Eds.) is especially helpful. For a penetrating analysis of life in the ghetto, see Kenneth B. Clark's, *Dark Ghetto* (1965).

An excellent discussion of the concept of race has been prepared by I. I. Gottesman (1968, pp. 11–51) in the book edited by Deutsch *et al.* UNESCO has also published a book, *Race and Science* (1961), that is helpful. *Science and the Concept of Race* (1968; Margaret Mead, T. Dobzhansky, Ethel Tobach, and R. E. Light, Eds.) provides additional useful information on this topic, as does Ashley Montagu's, *Race, Science, and Humanity* (1963).

Most of the empirical studies of the intelligence of blacks have been described in summary form by Audrey M. Shuey in her *The Testing of*

Negro Intelligence (1966). For a presentation and discussion of "jensenism," *Environment, Heredity, and Intelligence* (1969; A. R. Jensen *et al.*) should be consulted. Most "broad-band" books (see above) also present discussions of blacks' intelligence as well as useful reference lists on this topic. E. Earl Baughman's and W. Grant Dahlstrom's, *Negro and White Children: A Psychological Study in the Rural South* (1968), contains recent empirical findings on intelligence.

The scholastic performance of blacks is analyzed by Jensen *et al.* (1969) while empirical findings for a number of school subjects are presented by Baughman and Dahlstrom (1968). One of the most useful books in this domain is the one edited by Deutsch *et al.* (1968); this book contains several chapters on the education of disadvantaged youth as well as one on black performance in the desegregated school (by Irwin Katz). The reference lists in this book also serve as useful guides to additional reading on this topic. In addition, a number of valuable articles on the motivation and academic achievement of black Americans have been published in the summer, 1969 issue of *The Journal of Social Issues.* One article—by Patricia Gurin and her associates—focuses on the motivational dynamics of black youth with particular attention to the concept of internal versus external control as an important dimension of personality. In so doing, the authors advance a number of ideas which help to relate academic behavior to self-esteem.

Traditional thinking about black self-esteem, as well as critical reactions to this body of thought, may be found in *Negro Self-Concept: Implications for School and Citizenship* (1965; W. C. Kvaraceus *et al.*). Chapters by Erik H. Erikson and Robert Coles in the book edited by Parsons and Clark (1966) should also be consulted on this topic. Another very useful chapter in this domain has been written by Harold Proshansky and Peggy Newton (1968, pp. 178–218) for the volume edited by Deutsch *et al.* (1968). Although not readily available, dissertations by Marilyn M. Wendland (1967) and R. E. Bridgette (1970) contain a great deal of data pertaining to the self-esteem of southern blacks.

Anyone interested in rage and aggression should refer to W. H. Grier's and P. M. Cobbs's, *Black Rage* (1968). However, despite its title, this book also focuses upon a number of other psychological dimensions of black Americans. Hortense Powdermaker's article, "The Channeling of Negro Aggression by the Cultural Process" (1943), serves as a useful introduction to this topic, as does the second chapter in Pettigrew's book (1964).

With respect to the subject of psychopathology, the Grier–Cobbs book (1968) is again useful. A "must" book in this regard is A. Kardiner's and L. Ovesey's, *The Mark of Oppression: Explorations in the Personality of the American Negro* (1951). Based upon the psychoanalytic study of 25 blacks, this book is widely regarded as a classic. Probably the best statistical data in this domain are those which have been presented in a series of articles by B. Malzberg (1944, 1953, 1959). There are also many other articles that are helpful but not statistical; especially recommended are papers by D. P. Ausubel (1958), B. Dai (1956, pp. 545–566), Helen V. McLean (1949), Esther Milner (1953), and A. B. Sclare (1953). For an examination of the urban scene, consult S. Parker's and R. J. Kleiner's, *Mental Illness in the Urban Negro Community* (1965).

E. Franklin Frazier's, *The Negro Family in the United States* (1939), is generally considered to be the classic analysis of black family life. Jessie Bernard's, *Marriage and Family among Negroes* (1966), is a more recent examination of this subject. For statistical data, the U.S. Department of Labor's, *The Negro Family: The Case for National Action* (1965), is a valuable resource. For a penetrating examination of the black lower-class family, consult Lee Rainwater's chapter in the book edited by Parsons and Clark (1966). Finally, A. Billingsley's, *Black Families in White America* (1968), is an up-to-date "must" for individuals interested in this topic.

References

Adams, W. The Negro patient in psychiatric treatment. *American Journal of Orthopsychiatry*, 1950, **20**, 305-310.

Albee, G. W., *et al.* Statement by SPSSI on current IQ controversy: Heredity versus environment. *American Psychologist*, 1969, **24**, 1039-40.

Ausubel, D. P. Ego development among segregated Negro children. *Mental Hygiene*, 1958, **42**, 362-369.

Bandura, A., & Walters, R. H. *Social learning and personality development.* New York: Holt, Rinehart and Winston, 1963.

Baughman, E. E., & Dahlstrom, W. G. *Negro and white children: A psychological study in the rural South.* New York: Academic Press, 1968.

Bernard, J. *Marriage and family among Negroes.* Englewood Cliffs, N.J.: Prentice-Hall, 1966.

Billingsley, A. *Black families in white America.* Englewood Cliffs, N.J.: Prentice-Hall, 1968.

Bridgette, R. E. Self-esteem in Negro and white Southern adolescents. Unpublished Ph.D. dissertation, University of North Carolina at Chapel Hill, 1970.

Brieland, D. Black identity and the helping person. *Children*, 1969, **16**, 170-176.

Cattell, R. B. *The scientific analysis of personality.* Baltimore, Md.: Penguin, 1965.

Clark, K. B. *Dark ghetto: Dilemmas of social power.* New York: Harper & Row, 1965.

Clark, K. B., & Clark, M. P. Racial identification and preference in Negro children. In T. M. Newcomb and E. L. Hartley (Eds.), *Readings in social psychology.* New York: Holt, 1947.

Coleman, J. S., *et al. Equality of educational opportunities.* Washington, D. C.: U.S. Government Printing Office, 1966.

Coopersmith, S. *The antecedents of self-esteem.* San Francisco: Freeman, 1967.

Coopersmith, S. The development of self-esteem. In U.S. Department of Health, Education, and Welfare, *Perspectives on human deprivation: Biological, psychological, and sociological.* Washington, D. C.: U.S. Government Printing Office, 1968.

Crow, J. F. Genetic theories and influences: Comments on the value of diversity. *Harvard Educational Review,* 1969, **39**, 301-309.

Dai, B. Some problems of personality development among Negro children. In C. Kluckhohn, H. A. Murray, & D. M. Schneider (Eds.), *Personality: In nature, society and culture.* (2nd ed.) New York: Knopf, 1956.

Deutsch, M., Katz, I., & Jensen, A. R. (Eds.). *Social class, race, and psychological development.* New York: Holt, Rinehart and Winston, 1968.

Drake, St. C., & Cayton, H. R. *Black metropolis: A study of Negro life in a Northern city.* (Rev. ed.) New York: Harper & Row, 1962. 2 vols. (Originally published: 1945).

Dreger, R. M., & Miller, K. S. Comparative psychological studies of Negroes and whites in the United States. *Psychological Bulletin,* 1960, **57**, 361-402.

Dreger, R. M., & Miller, K. S. Comparative psychological studies of Negroes and whites in the United States: 1959-1965. *Psychological Bulletin Monograph Supplement,* 1968, **70** (3, Pt. 2).

Edson, L. jensenism, n. The theory that I.Q. is largely determined by the genes. *The New York Times Magazine,* August 31, 1969, p. 10.

Fitts, W. H. *Manual for the Tennessee self concept scale.* Nashville, Tenn.: Counselor Recordings and Tests, 1965.

Frazier, E. F. *The Negro family in the United States.* Chicago: University of Chicago Press, 1939. (Rev. ed., 1949.)

Frazier, E. F. *The Negro in the United States.* New York: Macmillan, 1949. (Rev. ed., 1957.)

Frazier, E. F. Problems and needs of Negro children and youth resulting from family disorganization. *Journal of Negro Education,* 1950, **19**, 269-277.

Frazier, E. F. *Black bourgeoisie.* New York: Collier, 1962.

Gibson, C. F. Concerning color. *Psychoanalytic Review,* 1931, **18**, 413-425.

Goodman, M. E. *Race awareness in young children.* Cambridge, Mass.: Addison-Wesley, 1952.

Gottesman, I. I. Biogenetics of race and class. In M. Deutsch, I. Katz, & A. R. Jensen (Eds.), *Social class, race, and psychological development.* New York: Holt, Rinehart and Winston, 1968.

Grambs, J. D. The self-concept: Basis for reeducation of Negro youth. In W. C. Kvaraceus, J. S. Gibson, F. Patterson, B. Seasholes, & J. D. Grambs, *Negro self-concept: Implications for school and citizenship.* New York: McGraw-Hill, 1965.

Grier, W. H., & Cobbs, P. M. *Black rage.* New York: Basic Books, 1968. (New York: Bantam, 1969, Paperback.)

Gurin, P., Gurin, G., Lao, R. C., & Beattie, M. Internal-external control in the motivational dynamics of Negro youth. *Journal of Social Issues,* 1969, **25**, 29-53.

Hammer, E. F. Frustration-aggression hypothesis extended to socio-racial areas: Comparison of Negro and white children's H-T-P's. *Psychiatric Quarterly*, 1953, **27**, 597-607.

Harrison, R. H., & Kass, E. H. Differences between Negro and white pregnant women on the MMPI. *Journal of Consulting Psychology*, 1967, **31**, 454-463.

Hess, R. D., Shipman, V., & Jackson, D. Early experience and the socialization of cognitive modes in children. *Child Development*, 1965, **36**, 869-886.

Hokanson, J. E., & Calden, G. Negro-white differences on the MMPI. *Journal of Clinical Psychology*, 1960, **16**, 32-33.

Hollingshead, A. B., & Redlich, F. C. *Social class and mental illness: A community study.* New York: Wiley, 1958.

Horowitz, R. E. Racial aspects of self-identification in nursery school children. *Journal of Psychology*, 1939, **7**, 91-99.

Hunt, J. McV. Environment, development, and scholastic achievement. In M. Deutsch, I. Katz, & A. R. Jensen (Eds.), *Social class, race, and psychological development.* New York: Holt Rinehart and Winston, 1968.

Hyman, H. H., & Reed, J. S. "Black matriarchy" reconsidered: Evidence from secondary analysis of sample surveys. *Public Opinion Quarterly*, 1969, **33**(3), 346-354.

Jensen, A. R. How much can we boost IQ and scholastic achievement? *Harvard Educational Review*, 1969, **39**, 1-123.

Jensen, A. R., Kagan, J. S., Hunt, J. McV., Crow, J. F., Bereiter, C., Elkind, D., Cronbach, L. J., & Brazziel, W. F. Environment, heredity, and intelligence. Cambridge, Mass.: *Harvard Educational Review*, 1969 (Reprint Series No. 2).

Jinks, J. L., & Fulker, D. W. Comparison of the biometrical genetical, MAVA, and classical approaches to the analysis of human behavior. *Psychological Bulletin*, 1970, **73**, 311-349.

Kagan, J. S., Hunt, J. McV., Crow, J. F., Bereiter, C., Elkind, D., Cronbach, L. J., & Brazziel, W. F. How much can we boost IQ and scholastic achievement? A discussion. *Harvard Educational Review*, 1969, **39**, 273-356.

Kamii, C. K. Socioeconomic class differences in the preschool socialization practices of Negro mothers. Unpublished Ph.D. dissertation, University of Michigan, 1965.

Kardiner, A., & Ovesey, L. *The mark of oppression: Explorations in the personality of the American Negro.* New York: Norton, 1951. (Cleveland, Ohio: World, 1962. Paperback.)

Katz, I. Factors influencing Negro performance in the desegregated school. In M. Deutsch, I. Katz, & A. R. Jensen (Eds.), *Social class, race, and psychological development.* New York: Holt, Rinehart and Winston, 1968.

Kennedy, W. A., Van de Riet, V., & White, J. C., Jr. A normative sample of intelligence and achievement of Negro elementary school children in the southeastern United States. *Monographs of the Society for Research in Child Development*, 1963, **28**, No. 90.

Kvaraceus, W. C., Gibson, J. S., Patterson, F., Seasholes, B., & Grambs, J. D. *Negro self-concept: Implications for school and citizenship.* New York: McGraw-Hill, 1965.

Landreth, C. & Johnson, B. C. Young children's responses to a picture and inset test designed to reveal reactions to persons of different skin color. *Child Development,* 1953, **24,** 63-79.

Lesser, G. S., Fifer, G., & Clark, D. H. Mental abilities of children from different social-class and cultural groups. *Monographs of the Society for Research in Child Development,* 1965, **30**(4).

Light, R. J., & Smith, P. V. Social allocation models of intelligence. *Harvard Educational Review,* 1969, **39,** 484-510.

Malcolm X (with A. Haley). *The autobiography of Malcolm X.* New York: Grove, 1965.

Malzberg, B. Mental disease among American Negroes: A statistical analysis. In O. Klineberg (Ed.), *Characteristics of the American Negro.* New York: Harper & Brothers, 1944.

Malzberg, B. Mental disease among Negroes in New York State, 1939-1941. *Mental Hygiene,* 1953, **37,** 450-476.

Malzberg, B. Mental disease among Negroes: An analysis of first admissions in New York State, 1949-1951. *Mental Hygiene,* 1959, **43,** 422-459.

McDonald, R. L., & Gynther, M. D. MMPI norms for Southern adolescent Negroes. *Journal of Social Psychology,* 1962, **58,** 277-282.

McDonald, R. L., & Gynther, M. D. Relationship of self and ideal-self descriptions with sex, race, and class in southern adolescents. *Journal of Personality and Social Psychology,* 1965, **1,** 85-88.

McLean, H. V. The emotional health of Negroes. *Journal of Negro Education,* 1949, **18,** 283-290.

Mead, M., Dobzhansky, T., Tobach, E., & Light, R. E. (Eds.). *Science and the concept of race.* New York: Columbia University Press, 1968.

Miller, E. W. *The Negro in America: A bibliography.* Cambridge, Mass.: Harvard University Press, 1966.

Milner, E. Some hypotheses concerning the influence of segregation on Negro personality development. *Psychiatry,* 1953, **16,** 291-297.

Montagu, A. *Race, science, and humanity.* Princeton, N. J.: Van Nostrand, 1963.

Mussen, P. H. Differences between the TAT responses of Negro and white boys. *Journal of Consulting Psychology,* 1953, **17,** 373-376.

Myers, J. K., & Roberts, B. H. *Social class, family dynamics, and mental illness.* New York: Wiley, 1959.

Myrdal, G. *An American dilemma: The Negro problem and modern democracy.* New York: Harper & Row, 1944. (20th Anniversary ed., 1962).

Parker, S., & Kleiner, R. J. *Mental illness in the urban Negro community.* New York: Free Press, 1965.

Parsons, T., & Clark, K. B. (Eds.). *The Negro American.* Boston: Houghton Mifflin, 1966.

Pettigrew, T. F. *A profile of the Negro American.* Princeton, N. J.: Van Nostrand, 1964.

Powdermaker, H. The channeling of Negro aggression by the cultural process. *American Journal of Sociology, 1943,* **48,** 750-758. Reprinted in C. Kluckhohn, H. A. Murray, & D. M. Schneider (Eds.), *Personality: In nature, society, and culture.* (2nd ed.) New York: Knopf, 1956.

Poverty: The war within the war. *Time Magazine,* May 13, 1966, p. 27.

Prange, A. J., Jr., & Vitols, M. M. Cultural aspects of the relatively low incidence of depression in southern Negroes. *International Journal of Social Psychiatry,* 1962, 8(2), 104-112.

Prange, A. J., Jr., & Vitols, M. M. Jokes among southern Negroes: The revelation of conflict. *Journal of Nervous and Mental Disease,* 1963, **136,** 162-166.

Proshansky, H., & Newton, P. The nature and meaning of Negro self-identity. In M. Deutsch, I. Katz, & A. R. Jensen (Eds.), *Social class, race, and psychological development.* New York: Holt, Rinehart and Winston, 1968.

Rosenthal, R., & Jacobson, L. Self-fulfilling prophecies in the classroom: Teachers' expectations as unintended determinants of pupils' intellectual competence. In M. Deutsch, I. Katz, & A. R. Jensen (Eds.), *Social class, race, and psychological development.* New York: Holt, Rinehart and Winston, 1968a.

Rosenthal, R., & Jacobson, L. *Pygmalion in the classroom: Teacher expectation and pupils' intellectual development.* New York: Holt, Rinehart and Winston, 1968b.

Sclare, A. Cultural determinants in the neurotic Negro. *British Journal of Medical Psychology,* 1953, **26,** 278-288.

Shuey, A. M. *The testing of Negro intelligence.* (2nd ed.). New York: Social Science Press, 1966.

Singer, S. L., & Stefflre, B. A note on racial differences in job values and desires. *Journal of Social Psychology,* 1956, **43,** 333-337.

Snow, R. E. Review of R. Rosenthal & L. Jacobson, *Pygmalion in the classroom: Teacher expectation and pupils' intellectual development. Contemporary Psychology,* 1969, **14,** 197-199.

St. Clair, H. R. Psychiatric interview experiences with Negroes. *American Journal of Psychiatry,* 1951, **108,** 113-119.

Stern, C. The biology of the Negro. *Scientific American,* 1954, **191**(4), 81-85.

Terman, L. M., & Merrill, M. A. *Measuring intelligence: A guide to the administration of the new revised Stanford-Binet tests of intelligence.* Boston: Houghton-Mifflin, 1937.

UNESCO. *Race and science.* New York: Columbia University Press, 1961.

U.S. Department of Health, Education, and Welfare. *Perspectives on human deprivation: Biological, psychological, and sociological.* Washington, D.C.: U.S. Government Printing Office, 1968.

U. S. Department of Labor. *The Negro family: The case for national action.* Washington, D. C.: U. S. Government Printing Office, 1965.

Wendland, M. M. Self-concept in Southern Negro and white adolescents as related to rural-urban residence. Unpublished Ph.D. dissertation, University of North Carolina at Chapel Hill, 1967.

Index

The letter n following a page number indicates that the entry is cited in a footnote to that page.

A

Abnormal behavior, *see* Psychopathology
Academic achievement, *see* Performance, scholastic
Achievement, *see* Performance, scholastic; Performance, nonscholastic
Achievement motivation
  relation to IQ change, 20
  see also Traits of children; Performance, scholastic; Socialization techniques
Activity level, *see* Traits of children
Adams, W., 75, 99
African culture, 2
Afro-American, *see* Race naming
Aggression, 56-64
  age differences, 62-63
  changes in, 1

channeling of, 57-60
denial of, 59
direct expression of, 58
displacement of, 58
economic reprisals, 57
emotional basis of, 61
empirical studies of, 61-64
genetic basis of, 60-61, 64
homicide rates, 58,61
identification with oppressor, 59
in African tribes, 61
in all-black communities, 61
in child training, 86-87
incidence of, 60-61
in drawings, 62-63
inhibition of, 57, 58, 64, 86-87
in humor, 58-59
in stories, 63-64
measurement of, 62
perceived in environment, 63, 64

Coleman, J. S., 25, 99
Coles, R., 96
Colored, *see* Race naming
Consistency, *see* Traits of children
Control, internal vs. external, 96
Cooperativeness, *see* Traits of children
Coopersmith, S., 43, 52, 54, 100
Counteraggression, 56, 58, 60, 64, 87, 94 n
Crime
  "white-man's-law," 66, 70
  see also Psychopathology, crime
Critcher, B., xix
Cronbach, L. J., 10, 101
Crow, J. F., 10, 100, 101
Cynicism, 50-51, 55, 91
  correlation with estrangement, 50 n
  measurement of, 49

D

Dahlstrom, W. G., viii, xii, xix, 2 n, 6, 8, 10, 12, 15, 16 n, 17, 19, 21, 22, 25 n, 26, 27, 30, 35 n, 36, 44, 63, 64, 71 n, 72, 78, 79, 80, 82, 88, 94, 96, 99
Dai, B., 97, 100
Dependency, *see* Traits of children
Depression, *see* Psychopathology
Desegregation of schools, xvi, 31-33, 92-94
  academic achievement, 31-32
  freedom-of-choice, 94
  "grade-per-year" plan, 93-94
  motivation, significance of, 31
  self-esteem, effect on, 33 n, 53-54, 93
  social acceptance, 31-32
  strategy for achieving, 32
  see also Education; Self-esteem
Deutsch, M., xii, 94, 95, 96, 100, 101, 103
Discrimination, xi, xii, xv, xvi, 3, 64, 69-70, 89, 90, 93

in therapy, 74
related to intelligence, 5
reversal of common pattern, 46
see also Religion
Dobzhansky, T., 95, 102
Dominance, 47-48
  parental dominance, 82
  see also Family; Socialization; Socialization techniques; Traits of children
Drake, St. C., 83, 100
Dreger, R. M., 5, 12, 95, 100
Drinking behavior, 83, 86 n
Drug addiction, *see* Psychopathology
Dyer, M., xix

E

Edson, L., 10, 100
Education, 92-94
  as preparation for urban life, 78
  compensatory programs, 9, 10
  deprivation of, 4
  preschool, 94
  see also Desegregation of schools; Headstart; Performance, scholastic
Effort expended on lessons, *see* Traits of children
Elkind, D., 10, 101
Ellison, R., xvii
Emotional expressiveness, *see* Traits of children
Emotional stability, *see* Traits of children
Encouragement, need for, *see* Traits of children
Environment and behavior, xv
Erikson, E. H., 55, 96
Estrangement, 50-51, 55
  correlation with cynicism, 50 n
  measurement of, 49
Evolution, xxi, 2

S

Schizophrenia, *see* Psychopathology, psychoses
Schneider, D. M., 100, 103
Scholastic performance, *see* Performance, scholastic
School desegregation, *see* Desegregation of schools; Education
Sclare, A., 97, 103
Seasholes, B., 40, 100, 101
Self-esteem, xii, 37-55
  advantage in being black, 46
  age, significance of, 53
  anecdotal evidence, 38
  athletic competition, effect of, 45
  blaming the "system," 45-46
  changes in, recent, 51
  childhood determinants, 43-45
  clinical evidence, 38
  compensatory mechanisms, 42
  definition of, 37
  desegregation, effect of, 45, 53-54, 93
  development of, 43-46
    in experience, 38
  empirical studies, 46-55
  internalization of others' attitudes, 38, 41
  Interpersonal Check List study, 47-48
  Jews,' 41
  measurement of, 52, 54
    race of examiner, 52
  quantitative-qualitative distinction, 41-42
  protection of, 61
  psychoanalytic findings, 38
  quantitative studies, 38-39
  Self-Esteem Inventory study, 52-55
    description of inventory, 52
  self/self-ideal discrepancy, 47-48
  sex differences, 49-50, 52-53
  situational factors, 53
  Tennessee Self Concept Scale study, 48-52
  traditional theory, 37-39
  traditional theory reconsidered, 39-46

  relationship to
    cynicism, 55
    estrangement, 55
    intelligence, 54
    parental behavior, 43-44, 54
    rural-urban residence, 45, 49-50
    social class, 48, 54-55
    whites,' 42
Self-fulfilling prophecy, 33-34
Sex behavior, xvi, 83
Shabazz, B., 4 n
Shipman, V., 86, 101
Shuey, A. M., xii, 5, 95, 103
Singer, S. L., 89, 103
Skin color, 38-40
Slavery, 2, 3, 37, 59, 60
  maternal socialization techniques, 86-87
  related to family life, 76-77
Smith, M. B., xiii
Smith, P. V., 10 n, 102
Snow, R. E., 34, 103
Social attitudes, *see* Discrimination
Social class, 1, 3-4
  related to
    black homogeneity, 12
    child training, 87 n
    crime, 66-67
    family life, 77, 83
    goals and aspirations, 88
    intelligence, 12
    intelligence tests, 11
    mental treatment, 74
    reinforcement, parental, 86
    scholastic performance, 30
    self-esteem, 43, 47, 48, 54-55
    submissiveness, 60
    white standards, 45 n
Socialization, 55, 76-89
  father absence, 85
  of aggression, 60,64
  preschool, 94
  see also Family; Socialization techniques
Socialization techniques, 84-89
  discrimination, reverse, 89